Apache Oozie Essentials

Unleash the power of Apache Oozie to create
and manage your Big Data and machine learning
pipelines in one go

Jagat Jasjit Singh

PUBLISHING

BIRMINGHAM - MUMBAI

Apache Oozie Essentials

First published: December 2015

Production reference: 1011215

Published by Packt Publishing Ltd.
Livery Place
35 Livery Street
Birmingham B3 2PB, UK.

ISBN 978-1-78588-038-4

www.packtpub.com

Credits

Author
Jagat Jasjit Singh

Reviewers
Siva Prakash

Rahul Tekchandani

Commissioning Editor
Dipika Gaonkar

Acquisition Editor
Tushar Gupta

Content Development Editor
Preeti Singh

Technical Editor
Dhiraj Chandanshive

Copy Editor
Roshni Banerjee

Project Coordinator
Shweta H Birwatkar

Proofreader
Safis Editing

Indexer
Priya Sane

Production Coordinator
Melwyn Dsa

Cover Work
Melwyn Dsa

About the Author

Jagat Jasjit Singh works for one of the largest telecom companies in Melbourne, Australia, as a big data architect. He has a total experience of over 10 years and has been working with the Hadoop ecosystem for more than 5 years. He is skilled in Hadoop, Spark, Oozie, Hive, Pig, Scala, machine learning, HBase, Falcon, Kakfa, GraphX, Flume, Knox, Sqoop, Mesos, Marathon, Chronos, Openstack, and Java. He has experience of a variety of Australian and European customer implementations. He actively writes on Big Data and IoT technologies on his personal blog (`http://jugnu.life`). Jugnu (a Punjabi word) is a firefly that glows at night and illuminates the world with its tiny light. Jagat believes in this same philosophy of sharing knowledge to make the world a better place. You can connect with him on LinkedIn at `https://au.linkedin.com/in/jagatsingh`.

All the (author side) earnings of this book will go towards charity. Please consider donating, if you have not purchased this book directly, at `http://www.pingalwara.net/donations.html`. You can donate with your PayPal account or credit card.

This book is dedicated to Almighty God, who gave me everything, my parents, and the wonderful people from the Omnia project at Commonwealth Bank of Australia (`https://github.com/CommBank`). I would like to acknowledge the help of Tushar Gupta, Dhiraj Chandanshive, Roshni Banerjee, and Preeti Singh from Packt Publishing in writing this book.

About the Reviewers

Siva Prakash has been working in the field of software development for the last 7 years. Currently, he is working with CISCO, Bangalore. He has an extensive development experience in desktop-, mobile-, and web-based applications in ERP, telecom, and the digital media industry. He has passion for learning new technologies and sharing knowledge thus gained with others. He has worked on big data technologies for the digital media industry. He loves trekking, travelling, music, reading books, and blogging.

He is available on LinkedIn at `https://www.linkedin.com/in/techsivam`.

Rahul Tekchandani is a Hadoop software developer who specializes in building and developing Hadoop data platforms for big financial institutions. With experience in software design, development, and support, he has engineered strong, data-driven applications using the Cloudera's Hadoop Distribution. Rahul has also worked as an information architect to support data sanitization and data governance.

Prior to his career in software development, he completed his masters in Management of Information Systems at University of Arizona and worked on academic projects for top tech and banking companies.

He currently lives in Charlotte, North Carolina. Visit his developer's blog at `www.rahultekchandani.com` to see what he is currently exploring, and to learn more about him.

www.PacktPub.com

Support files, eBooks, discount offers, and more

For support files and downloads related to your book, please visit www.PacktPub.com.

Did you know that Packt offers eBook versions of every book published, with PDF and ePub files available? You can upgrade to the eBook version at www.PacktPub.com and as a print book customer, you are entitled to a discount on the eBook copy. Get in touch with us at service@packtpub.com for more details.

At www.PacktPub.com, you can also read a collection of free technical articles, sign up for a range of free newsletters and receive exclusive discounts and offers on Packt books and eBooks.

https://www2.packtpub.com/books/subscription/packtlib

Do you need instant solutions to your IT questions? PacktLib is Packt's online digital book library. Here, you can search, access, and read Packt's entire library of books.

Why subscribe?

- Fully searchable across every book published by Packt
- Copy and paste, print, and bookmark content
- On demand and accessible via a web browser

Free access for Packt account holders

If you have an account with Packt at www.PacktPub.com, you can use this to access PacktLib today and view 9 entirely free books. Simply use your login credentials for immediate access.

Table of Contents

Preface

With the increasing popularity of Big Data in enterprise, every day more and more workloads are being shifted to Hadoop.

To run those regular processing jobs on Hadoop, we need a scheduler that can act as cron for all data pipelines. Oozie plays this role in the Big Data world.

This book introduces you to the world of Oozie using a step-by-step case study-based approach.

What this book covers

Chapter 1, Setting up Oozie, covers how to install and configure Oozie in Hadoop cluster. We will also learn how to install Oozie from the source code.

Chapter 2, My First Oozie Job, covers running a "Hello World" equivalent first Oozie job. It also introduces the concept of Workflow, Coordinator, and Bundles.

Chapter 3, Oozie Fundamentals, introduces the fundamental concepts of control nodes, expression language, web console, and running Oozie jobs from Hue.

Chapter 4, Running MapReduce Jobs, teaches how to run MapReduce jobs from Oozie and explores the concepts of Coordinators, Datasets, and cron-based frequency schedules.

Chapter 5, Running Pig Jobs, teaches how to run Pig jobs from Oozie. We will also cover the concept of parameterization of Datasets and Coordinator controls.

Chapter 6, Running Hive Jobs, introduces how to run Hive jobs and discusses the concepts of parameterization of Coordinator actions.

Chapter 7, Running Sqoop Jobs, shows how to run Sqoop jobs from Oozie and introduces the concept of HCatalog Datasets and EL functions.

Chapter 8, Running Spark Jobs, shows how to run Spark jobs. It also introduces the concept of Bundles and how they are used to group a set of Coordinator jobs.

Chapter 9, Running Oozie in Production, covers how to package the code for production deployments and how to rerun the jobs that have failed.

What you need for this book

To follow the tutorial and code examples in this book, you need to have access to Hadoop cluster or you can configure a single node virtual machine-based cluster. You should have a good laptop/desktop, preferably with a Linux operating system or Windows with VirtualBox installed.

Who this book is for

This book is for anyone who is familiar with basics of Hadoop and Hive, and now wants to automate the data and machine learning pipelines using Apache Oozie.

Conventions

In this book, you will find a number of text styles that distinguish between different kinds of information. Here are some examples of these styles and an explanation of their meaning.

Code words in text, database table names, folder names, filenames, file extensions, pathnames, dummy URLs, user input, and Twitter handles are shown as follows: "Now, edit the `torrc` file placed at the `/etc/tor/` directory."

Most of the code in the book is XML. A block of code is set as follows:

```xml
<workflow-app name="My_first_Workflow"
xmlns="uri:oozie:workflow:0.5">
  <start to="fs-2178"/>
  <kill name="Kill">
    <message>Action failed </message>
  </kill>
  <action name="fs-2178">
    <fs>
      <delete path='${nameNode}/user/hue'/>
```

```
      </fs>
      <ok to="End"/>
      <error to="Kill"/>
    </action>
    <end name="End"/>
  </workflow-app>
```

Any command-line input or output is written as follows:

```
# $ hadoop fs -ls /user/hue/learn_oozie
```

New terms and **important words** are shown in bold. Words that you see on the screen, for example, in menus or dialog boxes, appear in the text like this: "**Go to Settings | Networking | Port Forwarding** , Click on Add new port forwarding."

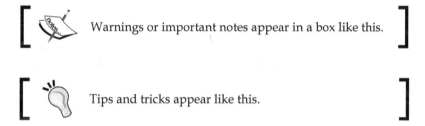

[Warnings or important notes appear in a box like this.]

[Tips and tricks appear like this.]

Reader feedback

Feedback from our readers is always welcome. Let us know what you think about this book—what you liked or disliked. Reader feedback is important for us as it helps us develop titles that you will really get the most out of.

To send us general feedback, simply e-mail feedback@packtpub.com, and mention the book's title in the subject of your message.

If there is a topic that you have expertise in and you are interested in either writing or contributing to a book, see our author guide at www.packtpub.com/authors.

Customer support

Now that you are the proud owner of a Packt book, we have a number of things to help you to get the most from your purchase.

Downloading the example code

You can download the example code files from your account at `http://www.packtpub.com` for all the Packt Publishing books you have purchased. If you purchased this book elsewhere, you can visit `http://www.packtpub.com/support` and register to have the files e-mailed directly to you.

Errata

Although we have taken every care to ensure the accuracy of our content, mistakes do happen. If you find a mistake in one of our books — maybe a mistake in the text or the code — we would be grateful if you could report this to us. By doing so, you can save other readers from frustration and help us improve subsequent versions of this book. If you find any errata, please report them by visiting `http://www.packtpub.com/submit-errata`, selecting your book, clicking on the **Errata Submission Form** link, and entering the details of your errata. Once your errata are verified, your submission will be accepted and the errata will be uploaded to our website or added to any list of existing errata under the Errata section of that title.

To view the previously submitted errata, go to `https://www.packtpub.com/books/content/support` and enter the name of the book in the search field. The required information will appear under the **Errata** section.

Piracy

Piracy of copyrighted material on the Internet is an ongoing problem across all media. At Packt, we take the protection of our copyright and licenses very seriously. If you come across any illegal copies of our works in any form on the Internet, please provide us with the location address or website name immediately so that we can pursue a remedy.

Please contact us at `copyright@packtpub.com` with a link to the suspected pirated material.

We appreciate your help in protecting our authors and our ability to bring you valuable content.

Questions

If you have a problem with any aspect of this book, you can contact us at `questions@packtpub.com`, and we will do our best to address the problem.

1
Setting up Oozie

Oozie is a workflow scheduler system to run Apache Hadoop jobs. Oozie Workflow jobs are **Directed Acyclic Graphs (DAGs)** of actions. More information on DAG can be found at `https://en.wikipedia.org/wiki/Directed_acyclic_graph`. Actions tell *what* to do in the job. Oozie supports running jobs of various types such as Java, Map-reduce, Pig, Hive, Sqoop, Spark, and Distcp. The output of one action can be consumed by the next action to create a chain sequence.

Oozie has client-server architecture, in which we install the server for storing the jobs and using client we submit our jobs to the server.

In this chapter, we will learn how to install Oozie for learning purpose and in production. For learning purposes, we will build Oozie from the source code, and for production we will use Hadoop distribution by Hortonworks. Throughout the book, we will use Hortonworks single node virtual machine. If you are using a different Hadoop distribution, you should not worry at all. All distribution packages are the same for Oozie software, which is made by the Apache community (`http://oozie.apache.org`).

After reading this chapter, we will be able to:

- Configure Oozie in Hortonworks distribution using Ambari
- Install Oozie using the source code provided as tar ball by the Apache Oozie website

Configuring Oozie in Hortonworks distribution

In this section, we will learn how to configure Oozie inside Hortonworks Hadoop distribution using Ambari. We will configure the Oozie server to use a MySQL database instead of the default Derby database to store all job information.

We will use a virtual machine to learn how to configure Oozie in Hortonworks Hadoop distribution. Most of other distributions, such as Cloudera, Pivotal, and so on, have similar steps.

Let's start with the following steps:

1. If you don't have VirtualBox on your machine, then download and install VirtualBox from `https://www.virtualbox.org/wiki/Downloads`.

2. Download the Hortonworks single node virtual machine from `http://hortonworks.com/hdp/downloads/`. It will take 1-2 hours depending upon your Internet connection speed.

 It is always good to store the virtual machine images in a common folder. For example, I have folder in my machine such as `~/dev/vm/`. It makes virtual machine image management easier.

3. After the download is complete, open the VirtualBox and click on **File | Import Appliance**:

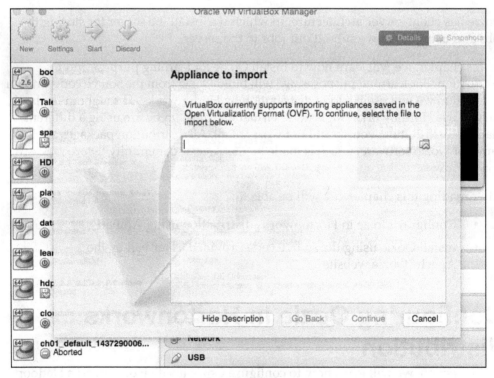

Import appliance

4. Click on the **Import Appliance** button, browse to the place where you downloaded the virtual machine image, and then click on **Continue**.

5. Wait till the VirtualBox imports the new machine.

6. Once you can see the machine is imported, click on **Start machine** in the virtual machine console.

7. On completion of boot process of the machine, you can log in to the Ambari dashboard by opening the URL `http://127.0.0.1:8080` in your browser.

8. Use the username as well as password as `admin`.

   It will take some time for all services to start up and report their status to Ambari. Once the system has reported the status, all services have a glance at the Ambari console. It is also a good idea to stop the services which we are not using to reduce the load on the system.

9. In the Ambari dashboard, click on the link named **Oozie** on the left side. You can see there are two components for Oozie, **Oozie Server** and **Oozie Client**. Since we are using a single node cluster, we have both the server and client installed on the same machine. In the production environment, you will configure the Oozie server and clients separately on different machines. Using the client, we will submit the jobs to server. Before submitting the job, we will tell where the server is located using the `OOZIE_URL` variable.

> To save time in manually specifying the Oozie server on the client machine every time, you can set the environment variable `OOZIE_URL` in your `bash_profile` or `environment` file depending on the operating system you use. You should say export `OOZIE_URL=http://oozieserver:11000/oozie;` in this book `oozieserver` will be localhost.

10. Now click on the **Config link** at the top and we will configure the database as MySQL. The Oozie server will use MySQL to store the job information:

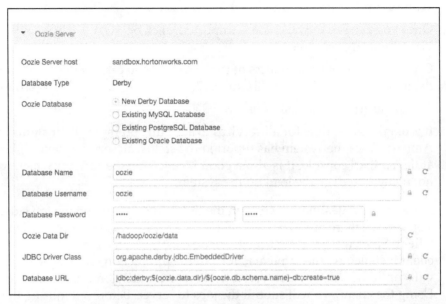

Ambari Oozie configuration

11. You may notice, at this moment, the server has been configured to use a Derby database. Derby is good for playing and testing, but not for running the production sever. We will configure it to use a MySQL-based database.

12. Log in to the virtual machine using SSH as follows:

```
$ ssh root@127.0.0.1 -p 2222
```

The default password is hadoop.

13. After you log in to the SSH session, log in to MySQL:

```
$ mysql -u root
```

14. Since this is a test virtual machine, the password is not configured. In production, you will be having password protection.

15. At the MySQL prompt, execute the following SQL statements:

```
CREATE USER 'oozie'@'%' IDENTIFIED BY 'hadoop';

CREATE DATABASE oozie;

GRANT ALL PRIVILEGES ON oozie.* TO 'oozie'@'%' WITH GRANT
OPTION;
```

The following output will be generated:

```
● ● ●                learn_oozie — root@sandbox:~ — ssh — 90×27
owners.

Type 'help;' or '\h' for help. Type '\c' to clear the current input statement.

mysql> show databases;
+--------------------+
| Database           |
+--------------------+
| information_schema |
| hive               |
| mysql              |
| ranger             |
| ranger_audit       |
| test               |
+--------------------+
6 rows in set (0.47 sec)

mysql> CREATE USER 'oozie'@'%' IDENTIFIED BY 'hadoop';
Query OK, 0 rows affected (0.01 sec)

mysql> CREATE DATABASE oozie;
Query OK, 1 row affected (0.00 sec)

mysql> GRANT ALL PRIVILEGES ON oozie.* TO 'oozie'@'%' WITH GRANT OPTION;
Query OK, 0 rows affected (0.01 sec)

mysql> █
```

Oozie database creation

16. To make Oozie work with MySQL, we need to get driver for it. Let's download the MySQL JDBC driver from the MySQL JDBC jar download section. Extract the jar to a folder such as /root/mysql inside the virtual machine:

```
$ cd ~/

$ mkdir mysql

$ cd mysql

$ # Download the MySQL JDBC Driver

$ wget http://dev.mysql.com/get/Downloads/Connector-J/mysql-
connector-java-5.1.36.tar.gz

$ # Extract tar

$ tar -xvf mysql-connector-java-5.1.36.tar.gz

$ # Tell Ambari that we got new MYSQL JDBC driver which it can
use

$ ambari-server setup --jdbc-db=mysql --jdbc-
driver=/root/mysql/mysql-connector-java-5.1.36/mysql-
connector-java-5.1.36-bin.jar
```

17. In the Ambari dashboard, configure the MySQL database with the following details:

Field name	Value
Database Name	oozie
Database Username	oozie
Database Password	hadoop
JDBC Driver Class	com.mysql.jdbc.Driver
JDBC Database URL	jdbc:mysql://localhost:3306/${oozie.db. schema.name}?createDatabaseIfNotExist=true

18. In the Ambari dashboard page, click on **Test Connection**. If all is good, there should be a green tick. So, we have now configured the Oozie server to use MySQL database instead of Derby.

19. Finally, to confirm that Oozie works properly, in another browser tab open the Oozie dashboard by entering the URL http://127.0.0.1:11000/oozie.

This completes the first section in which we learned how to configure Oozie for Hortonworks Ambari distribution.

Installing Oozie using tar ball

In this section, we will learn how to build and install Oozie from the source code. Since Hortonworks virtual machine had already Oozie installed, we did not need to do anything.

Just to learn how to install Oozie from tar ball in this section, we will use a Vagrant-based machine in which we will configure and install the Oozie server.

The summary of the steps we will perform is as follows:

1. Create a test build machine.
2. Download and build the Oozie code to make a WAR file.
3. Download the Oozie third-party dependency jars and libraries.
4. Package the Oozie WAR file and its dependencies into a WAR file.
5. Configure the MySQL database for the Oozie server.
6. Configure the shared library.
7. Start and test the Oozie server.

Just as a heads-up, the vagrant machine needs lot of resources to build the code. So, if you do not have a powerful machine, you can build it directly on your host operating system rather than the virtual machine. I am working on a MacBook Pro, which has a 16 GB RAM. I gave 8 GB to the virtual machine to show how to install Oozie from source.

Creating a test virtual machine

The following are the steps to create a test virtual machine:

1. Download latest Oozie distribution from the Apache Oozie website. Go to the downloads section and download the latest version (4.2.0 at time of writing) in machine where you want to install it.

2. Download and install Vagrant depending upon your operating system:

The Vagrant download

3. After this, go to the VirtualBox website. Depending on your computer operating system, download and install the VirtualBox.

4. If you already have a test machine that has a Linux-based operating system, then you can skip the Vagrant-based setup and follow the steps for building Oozie from scripts.

5. Clone the source code for the book from `https://github.com/jagatsingh/apache_oozie_essentials.git`.

6. Create a folder in your system called `dev`, or any suitable location where we can clone code. We will call the `dev/apache_oozie_essentials` location as `<BOOK_CODE_HOME>` in this book. The following are the commands to do this:

```
$ git clone
https://github.com/jagatsingh/apache_oozie_essentials.git
$ cd <BOOK_CODE_HOME>
$ cd learn_oozie/ch01
$ # Let's start the virtual machine
$ vagrant up
```

7. Wait for some time till our new test machine comes up.

   Here is what Vagrant does behind the scene:

   ○ Gets the image of the Centos 6.5 operating system
   ○ Installs JDK, MySQL, Git, and Maven

8. All the preceding steps are being done by the provider script, which is shown as follows:

```
$ sudo wget http://repos.fedorapeople.org/repos/dchen/apache-
maven/epel-apache-maven.repo -O /etc/yum.repos.d/epel-apache-
maven.repo
$ sudo yum install -y java-1.7.0-openjdk mysql-server git
unzip zip apache-maven telnet
$ cp /vagrant/files/maven/settings.xml /etc/maven/
$ sudo service mysqld start
```

9. When the machine starts off completely, you will see something, as shown in the following figure:

```
● ● ●                    ch01 — bash — 90×30
==> default: OK
==> default: Filling help tables...
==> default: OK
==> default:
==> default: To start mysqld at boot time you have to copy
==> default: support-files/mysql.server to the right place for your system
==> default: PLEASE REMEMBER TO SET A PASSWORD FOR THE MySQL root USER !
==> default: To do so, start the server, then issue the following commands:
==> default:
==> default: /usr/bin/mysqladmin -u root password 'new-password'
==> default: /usr/bin/mysqladmin -u root -h ranga.wg.dir.telstra.com password 'new-passwor
d'
==> default:
==> default: Alternatively you can run:
==> default: /usr/bin/mysql_secure_installation
==> default: which will also give you the option of removing the test
==> default: databases and anonymous user created by default.  This is
==> default: strongly recommended for production servers.
==> default:
==> default: See the manual for more instructions.
==> default: You can start the MySQL daemon with:
==> default: cd /usr ; /usr/bin/mysqld_safe &
==> default: You can test the MySQL daemon with mysql-test-run.pl
==> default: cd /usr/mysql-test ; perl mysql-test-run.pl
==> default:
==> default: Please report any problems with the /usr/bin/mysqlbug script!
==> default: [  OK  ]
==> default: Starting mysqld:
==> default: [  OK  ]
jagats-mbp:ch01 jagatsingh$ 
```

Vagrant up finish

If you need a quick tutorial on how Vagrant works, then read the documentation on Vagrant at https://docs.vagrantup.com/v2/.

10. Now we can log in to the virtual machine by using the command `vagrant ssh`. This command should be executed from the folder `ch01`.

11. Inside the Vagrant virtual machine, **mount/vagrant** is same as the `ch01` folder, placed at <BOOK_CODE_HOME>/learn_oozie/, from where we started the Vagrant.

```
$ cd /vagrant
$ ls
```

Building Oozie source code

Let's build Oozie from the source code. We will download the latest Oozie distribution and build it. All of these steps are present in the script `build_oozie.sh` placed at `cat/vagrant/scripts/`.

The contents of the script which we will run is as follows:

```
# Download and make Oozie distribution
$ cd ~/
$ mkdir {oozie_build,oozie_install,hadoop_install}
$ cd oozie_build
$ wget
http://apache.mirror.digitalpacific.com.au/oozie/4.2.0/oozie-
4.2.0.tar.gz
$ tar -xvf oozie-4.2.0.tar.gz
$ cd oozie-4.2.0
$ bin/mkdistro.sh -DskipTests -P hadoop-2
```

Summary of the build script

In the `oozie_build` directory, we will build Oozie. In the `oozie_install` directory, we will install Oozie. In the `hadoop_install` directory, we will download Hadoop distribution and copy few jars needed for Oozie to run. You can also download the jars from your own hadoop cluster.

Let's run the command to start the Oozie build. It will take some time to download all the dependencies and build the source code:

```
$ /vagrant/scripts/build_oozie.sh
```

 If you already have a Maven repository on your host machine and want to to avoid downloading maven artifacts again, then look at the Maven settings file. I have configured (and commented) it to use my MacBook home maven as I already had all the artifacts there. You can uncomment that if you want to do something similar.

Codehaus Maven move

Codehaus no longer serves up Maven repositories, we need to configure Maven to download those dependencies from a different location. If you look at /etc/maven/settings.xml, which came with this machine, it has already been modified. You can see the details about it on the Codehaus website at http://www.codehaus.org/mechanics/maven/.

On a successful build, you should see something like the following screenshot:

Oozie build success

Download dependency jars

To run Oozie properly, the Oozie WAR file needs to have some dependencies packaged with it. Some of them are Hadoop, MySQL JDBC driver, Ext-js, and so on. The MySQL JDBC driver is used by the server database, and Ext-js is used by the Oozie web console.

We will copy all of them in to one folder, libext, and then use the oozie-setup.sh command to build the WAR file.

Let's download the Hadoop jars from your cluster or by executing the following steps:

```
$ cd ~/hadoop_install
$ wget https://archive.apache.org/dist/hadoop/common/hadoop-
2.4.0/hadoop-2.4.0.tar.gz
$ tar -xvf hadoop-2.4.0.tar.gz
```

Now we should have Hadoop extracted to the folder `~/hadoop_install`.

The preceding steps can be executed in one go using the following command:

```
/vagrant/scripts/download_hadoop_jars.sh
```

Preparing to create a WAR file

To create the WAR file, we need to copy the Oozie distro built earlier and combine it with the jars for Hadoop, the MySQL JDBC driver, and the Ext-js library.

If you remember from the previous Ambari Oozie configuration, we used MySQL as our database and configured it using the `ambari-setup` command. We will take a similar approach for the MySQL JDBC driver jar, which we are providing by merging it with the Oozie WAR file.

Let's prepare the Oozie distro using the following commands:

```
# Prepare to make Oozie war file
$ cd ~/oozie_install
$ cp ~/oozie_build/oozie-4.2.0/distro/target/oozie-4.2.0-
distro.tar.gz ~/oozie_install
$ tar -xvf oozie-4.2.0-distro.tar.gz
$ cd oozie-4.2.0
$ # Removing hsql jar as they cause class conflict
$ rm lib/hsqldb-1.8.0.10.jar
```

Download the MySQL jar using the following commands:

```
# Collect all external jar files
$ mkdir libext
$ wget https://dev.mysql.com/get/Downloads/Connector-J/mysql-
connector-java-5.1.36.tar.gz --no-check-certificate
$ tar -xvf mysql-connector-java-5.1.36.tar.gz
$ # Copy MySQL JDBC Driver
$ cp mysql-connector-java-5.1.36/*.jar libext/
```

Merge the Hadoop jars and the ext-js library using the following commands:

```
$ cd libext
$ wget http://dev.sencha.com/deploy/ext-2.2.zip
$ # Collect hadoop related jars
$ shopt -s globstar
$ /bin/cp -rf ~/hadoop_install/hadoop-2.4.0/share/**/*.jar
~/oozie_install/oozie-4.2.0/libext
$ # Removing source jars to reduce size
$ rm -rf *sources*
$ rm -rf *jasper*
```

All of the preceding steps can be executed in one go using the following command:

/vagrant/scripts/war_file_preparation.sh

After successful execution, go to /home/vagrant/oozie_install/oozie-4.2.0/ libext and see that we now have jars placed in the folder.

Create a WAR file

Now we need to package the oozie-distro and jars that we copied in to the libext folder as a single packaged WAR file. This WAR file will be deployed in tomcat by going to the folder /home/vagrant/oozie_install/oozie-4.2.0 and executing the following command:

bin/oozie-setup.sh prepare-war

The command completes with a WAR file being created in the folder, as shown in the following screenshot:

```
INFO: Adding extension: /home/vagrant/oozie_install/oozie-4.2.0/libext/tomcat-coyote.jar
INFO: Adding extension: /home/vagrant/oozie_install/oozie-4.2.0/libext/tomcat-dbcp.jar
INFO: Adding extension: /home/vagrant/oozie_install/oozie-4.2.0/libext/tomcat-i18n-es.jar
INFO: Adding extension: /home/vagrant/oozie_install/oozie-4.2.0/libext/tomcat-i18n-fr.jar
INFO: Adding extension: /home/vagrant/oozie_install/oozie-4.2.0/libext/tomcat-i18n-ja.jar
INFO: Adding extension: /home/vagrant/oozie_install/oozie-4.2.0/libext/tomcat-juli.jar
INFO: Adding extension: /home/vagrant/oozie_install/oozie-4.2.0/libext/xmlenc-0.52.jar
INFO: Adding extension: /home/vagrant/oozie_install/oozie-4.2.0/libext/xz-1.0.jar
INFO: Adding extension: /home/vagrant/oozie_install/oozie-4.2.0/libext/zookeeper-3.4.5.jar

New Oozie WAR file with added 'ExtJS library, JARs' at /home/vagrant/oozie_install/oozie-4.2.0/oozie-server/webapps/oozie.war

INFO: Oozie is ready to be started

[vagrant@localhost oozie-4.2.0]$ pwd
/home/vagrant/oozie_install/oozie-4.2.0
[vagrant@localhost oozie-4.2.0]$ bin/oozie-setup.sh prepare-war
```

Prepare a WAR file

Exercise: Execute `bin/oozie-setup.sh` help and read all the commands possible with the `setup` command.

Configure Oozie MySQL database

If you remember, we configured Ambari Oozie to use MySQL database for Oozie. We will do the same for this instance of the Oozie server.

At the Mysql prompt, execute the following:

```
$ mysql -u root
CREATE USER 'oozie'@'%' IDENTIFIED BY 'hadoop';
CREATE DATABASE oozie;
GRANT ALL PRIVILEGES ON oozie.* TO 'oozie'@'%' WITH GRANT OPTION;
```

This will create the Oozie database, which will be used by the server.

Go to `/home/vagrant/oozie_install/oozie-4.2.0/conf` and open the `oozie-site.xml` file. In this file, all the Oozie settings are declared. All the Oozie configuration properties and their default values are defined in the `oozie-default.xml` file.

Oozie resolves configuration property values in the following order.

If a `Java System` property is defined, it uses its value, else if the Oozie configuration file (`oozie-site.xml`) contains the property, it uses its value, else it uses the default value documented in the `oozie-default.xml` file.

 Oozie does not use the `oozie-default.xml` file found in the `conf/` directory. It is there for reference purposes only.

Let's edit the `oozie-site.xml` and configure the database details. You can use the vi editor or copy the settings from the already created file using the following command:

```
$ cp /vagrant/files/oozie/oozie-site.xml
/home/vagrant/oozie_install/oozie-4.2.0/conf/
```

If you want to edit it manually, then add the following code:

```
<property>
   <name>oozie.service.JPAService.jdbc.driver</name>
   <value>com.mysql.jdbc.Driver</value>
```

```
    <description>JDBC driver class</description>
</property>
<property>
    <name>oozie.service.JPAService.jdbc.url</name>
    <value>jdbc:mysql://localhost:3306/${oozie.db.schema.name}?
createDatabaseIfNotExist=true</value>
    <description>JDBC URL</description>
</property>
<property>
    <name>oozie.service.JPAService.jdbc.username</name>
    <value>oozie</value>
    <description>DB user name</description>
</property>
<property>
    <name>oozie.service.JPAService.jdbc.password</name>
    <value>hadoop</value>
    <description>DB user password</description>
</property>
```

 Exercise: Execute bin/ooziedb.sh help and read all the commands possible with the setup command.

Let's create the database tables in our newly created database using the following command:

bin/ooziedb.sh create -sqlfile oozie.sql -run

The following screenshot shows the output generated:

```
[vagrant@localhost oozie-4.2.0]$ bin/ooziedb.sh create -run
  setting CATALINA_OPTS="$CATALINA_OPTS -Xmx1024m"

Validate DB Connection
DONE
DB schema does not exist
Check OOZIE_SYS table does not exist
DONE
Create SQL schema
DONE
Create OOZIE_SYS table
DONE

Oozie DB has been created for Oozie version '4.2.0'


The SQL commands have been written to: /tmp/ooziedb-6751666195906463768.sql
[vagrant@localhost oozie-4.2.0]$
```

Database creation success

Configure the shared library

We just need to tell Oozie about the shared libraries before starting the Oozie server. The Oozie `sharelib .tar.gz` file bundled with the distribution contains the necessary files to run Oozie Map-reduce streaming, Pig, Hive, Sqoop, Hcatalog, and Distcp actions.

Let's execute the following command:

```
bin/oozie-setup.sh sharelib create -fs oozie-sharelib-4.2.0.tar.gz
```

The following screenshot shows the output generated:

```
[vagrant@localhost oozie-4.2.0]$ ls
bin    data    lib    libtools  mysql-connector-java-5.1.36          oozie-client-4.2.0.tar.gz  oozie-examples.tar.gz  oozie-sharelib-4.2.0.tar.gz
conf   docs.zip  libext  logs     mysql-connector-java-5.1.36.tar.gz  oozie-core                 oozie-server           oozie.sql
[vagrant@localhost oozie-4.2.0]$ bin/oozie-setup.sh sharelib create -fs oozie-sharelib-4.2.0.tar.gz
  setting CATALINA_OPTS="$CATALINA_OPTS -Xmx1024m"
SLF4J: Class path contains multiple SLF4J bindings.
SLF4J: Found binding in [jar:file:/home/vagrant/oozie_install/oozie-4.2.0/lib/slf4j-simple-1.6.6.jar!/org/slf4j/impl/StaticLoggerBinder.class]
SLF4J: Found binding in [jar:file:/home/vagrant/oozie_install/oozie-4.2.0/lib/slf4j-log4j12-1.6.6.jar!/org/slf4j/impl/StaticLoggerBinder.class]
SLF4J: Found binding in [jar:file:/home/vagrant/oozie_install/oozie-4.2.0/libext/slf4j-log4j12-1.7.5.jar!/org/slf4j/impl/StaticLoggerBinder.class]
SLF4J: See http://www.slf4j.org/codes.html#multiple_bindings for an explanation.
SLF4J: Actual binding is of type [org.slf4j.impl.SimpleLoggerFactory]
the destination path for sharelib is: /user/vagrant/share/lib/lib_20150719103405
[vagrant@localhost oozie-4.2.0]$
```

Create a shared library

Start server testing and verification

The following command is used to start the server:

```
bin/oozied.sh start
```

 Exercise: Execute `bin/oozied.sh` help and read all the commands possible with the `setup` command.

The command, on successful completion, will not print any error message. We can check the status of Oozie server using the following command:

```
bin/oozie admin -oozie http://localhost:11000/oozie -status
```

The output should be:

```
system mode: NORMAL
```

We can also check the Oozie web console by opening the URL `http://localhost:11000/oozie`.

Summary

We started this chapter with the configuration of Oozie inside the Hortonworks virtual machine. We learned how to configure the database for Oozie. Then we started building Oozie from the source code. We packaged the WAR file and also configured the MySQL database.

This completes the installation for the Oozie server.

In the next chapter, we will run our first Oozie job. We will learn how to run Hadoop filesystem commands in Oozie. We will also install Hue and create our Workflow using the editor provided by it.

2
My First Oozie Job

In this chapter, we will dive in the world of Oozie by running our first Oozie job. We will also set up Hue, which will allow us to edit Oozie Workflows from a graphical user interface. We will be using the Hortonworks VirtualBox machine to do all our projects throughout the book.

In this chapter, we will do the following:

- Install and configure Hue Oozie Workflow editor
- Run our first Oozie Workflow job
- Understand the concept of Workflow, Coordinator, and Bundles
- Understand Oozie Fs actions
- Use Oozie console to see the job status
- Use the Oozie command line to get the job status

Installing and configuring Hue

The Hortonworks virtual machine already has one version of Hue running, but that is very old. We will install the latest version of Hue ourselves since it has a better Oozie editor.

Start the virtual machine. Once the machine is up and running, we can log in to that via SSH using the following command:

```
$ ssh root@127.0.0.1 -p 2222
```

The default password is hadoop.

Let's download and configure Hue. Here are the steps to do so:

1. Download the latest release of Hue.
2. Install the dependencies required to build Hue via yum.
3. Build the Hue package using the `make` command.
4. Before you execute the following commands, check the Hue website (`http://gethue.com/category/release/`) and find out the latest version of Hue. I have used 3.8.1 in this book. But I suggest you to download the latest one. The only change needed in the following is to change the version 3.8.1 to whatever latest version is present:

```
$ mkdir -p /opt/learn_oozie/hue

$ chmod 777 /opt/learn_oozie/hue

$ chown hue:hue /opt/learn_oozie/hue

$ sudo su hue

$ cd /opt/learn_oozie/hue

$ # Download Hue

$ wget https://dl.dropboxusercontent.com/u/730827/
hue/releases/3.8.1/hue-3.8.1.tgz

$ tar -xvf hue-3.8.1.tgz

$ cd hue-3.8.1

$ Install dependencies required to build Hue

$ yum install ant asciidoc cyrus-sasl-devel cyrus-sasl-gssapi
gcc gcc-c++ krb5-devel libtidy  libxml2-devel libxslt-devel
make mysql mysql-devel openldap-devel python-devel sqlite-
devel openssl-devel gmp-devel

$ Build Hue

$ make apps
```

5. Wait for some time for Hue to get ready. You can also run the following scripts to do all the steps in one go:

```
<BOOK_CODE_HOME>/ch02/scripts/install_hue.sh
```

Once it is successful, you will get following message:

```
Post-processed 'zookeeper/art/line_icons.png' as
'zookeeper/art/line_icons.f50a9ca444bf.png'

Post-processed 'zookeeper/art/icon_zookeeper_24.png' as
'zookeeper/art/icon_zookeeper_24.e3168d30a559.png'

Post-processed 'zookeeper/help/index. ml'
```

```
Post-processed 'zookeeper/css/zookeehtml' as
'zookeeper/help/index.7570dbb625f3.htper.css' as
'zookeeper/css/zookeeper.dab3cbab10bb.css'
```

```
Post-processed 'zookeeper/js/base64.js' as
'zookeeper/js/base64.ce5e02af31e5.js'
```

```
576 static files copied to '/opt/learn_oozie/hue/hue-
3.8.1/build/static', 576 post-processed.
```

```
make[1]: Leaving directory `/opt/learn_oozie/hue/hue-
3.8.1/apps'[hue@sandbox hue-3.8.1]$
```

> To save time in copying files from host machine to guest and vice versa, I have configured my host machine's Home folder as shared folder with guest. You can also do the same.

We need to start Hue now, but before that we need to make few changes to the Hue configuration file, hue.ini.

Following are the steps to make the changes and start Hue:

1. The default port of Hue, 8888, is already used in this virtual machine. So we will change the port for Hue in our machine.

2. Open the file in vi or your favorite editor and enter the following command:

   `$ vi desktop/conf/hue.in`

3. Change the port from 8888 to 18888.

   There are few other changes related to hue.ini in which we need to change the hostname to sandbox.hortonworks.com. I have already done those changes in the hue.ini file. So you can just copy it from following location:

   `<BOOK_CODE_HOME>/ch02/files/hue/hue.ini`

   We need to add one port forwarding to see the Hue web page in the host machine.

4. Open running VirtualBox.

5. Go to **Settings** | **Networking** | **Port Forwarding**. Click on **Add new port forwarding rule**.

6. Add one more entry to forward port `8888` on guest to host at `18888`, as shown in the following screenshot:

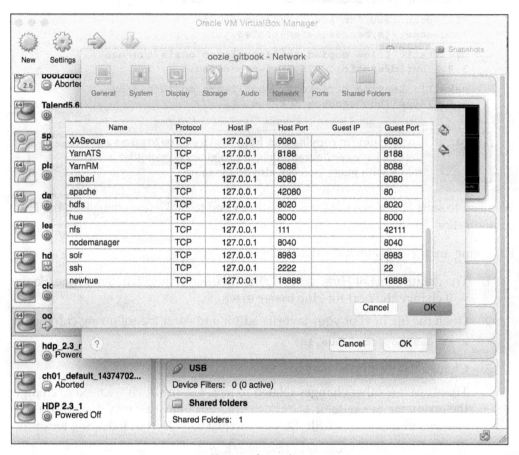

Hue port forwarding

7. Let's start Hue using the following commands:

    ```
    $ sudo su hue
    $ cd /opt/learn_oozie/hue/hue-3.8.1
    $ build/env/bin/supervisor
    ```

    Once this is successful, you will get the following message:

    ```
    [hue@sandbox hue-3.8.1]$ build/env/bin/supervisor

    [INFO] Not running as root, skipping privilege drop

    starting server with options {'ssl_certificate': None,
    'workdir': None, 'server_name': 'localhost', 'host':
    '0.0.0.0', 'daemonize': False, 'threads': 40, 'pidfile': None,
    ```

```
'ssl_private_key': None, 'server_group': 'hue',
'ssl_cipher_list':'DEFAULT:!aNULL:!eNULL:!LOW:!EXPORT:!SSLv2',
'port': 18888, 'server_user': 'hue'}
```

8. On the host machine, use your browser and open the URL
   `http://127.0.0.1:18888/`.

9. Pick up any username and password for first login. I have chosen `hue` for
   both username and password.

 Take some time to browse the Hue interface. Hue has lots of
functionality we can run, such as Hive, Pig, and Oozie jobs.

We are interested in the Workflow editor functionality, where we can edit and watch
the Oozie jobs. Click on **Workflows** and take some time to see what Hue provides.

 This often happens with me! Learning new things make me forget the
basics. So, if you need, have a quick refresher for XSD by referring to
the following links:

`http://www.w3schools.com/schema`

`http://www.w3schools.com/xml/default.asp`

Oozie concepts

Before we move further, let's look at a few basic concepts of Oozie. In each chapter,
we will take some time to learn some new concepts of Oozie besides looking at
working examples.

Workflows

Workflow tells Oozie what to do. They are the DAG (`https://en.wikipedia.org/
wiki/Directed_acyclic_graph`) representation of actions (tasks). It is a collection
of actions arranged in required dependency graph. As a part of Workflow's
definition, we write some actions and call them in a certain order.

These are of various types for tasks that we can do as a part of the Workflow, for
example, Fs (Hadoop filesystem) action, Pig action, Hive action, MapReduce action,
Spark action, and so on. We will discuss Fs action in this chapter.

Coordinator

Coordinator tells Oozie *when* to do a task, for example, *when* is the component in Oozie world decided by time or *when* is the given input data set available. We will discuss the Coordinators later in this book.

Bundles

Bundles tell Oozie what all things to do together as a group, for example, a set of Coordinators that can be run together to satisfy a given business requirement can be combined as Bundle.

Book case study

Throughout this book, we will try to solve case study that will revolve around various concepts of Oozie.

One of the main use cases of Hadoop is ETL data processing.

Suppose we work for a large consulting company and have won a project to set up a Big Data cluster inside the customer data center. On a high level, the requirements are to set up an environment that will satisfy the following flow:

1. Get data from various sources in Hadoop (file-based loads and Sqoop-based loads).
2. Preprocess them with various scripts (Pig, Hive, and MapReduce).
3. Insert that data into Hive tables for use by analysts and data scientists.
4. Data scientists then write machine learning models (Spark).

We will use Oozie as our processing scheduling system to do all the preceding tasks. Since writing actual Hive, Sqoop, MapReduce, Pig, and Spark code is not in the scope of this book, I will not dive into explaining business logic for those. So I have kept them very simple.

In our architecture, we have one landing server that sits outside as the front door of the cluster. All source systems send files to us via scp and we regularly (for example, nightly to keep it simple) push them to HDFS using the `hadoop fs -copyFromLocal` command. This script is cron-driven. It has a very simple business logic: run every night at 8:00 P.M. and move all the files that it sees on the landing server into HDFS.

The work of Oozie starts from this point:

1. Oozie picks the file and cleans it using Pig Script to replace all the delimiters, from comma (,) to pipes (|). We will write the same code using Pig and MapReduce.

2. Then, push those processed files into a Hive table.

3. For different source systems which are database-based MySQL tables, we do nightly Sqoop when the load of the database is light. So, we extract all the records that have been generated on the previous business day.

4. We insert the output of that too into Hive tables.

5. Analyst and data scientists write there magical Hive scripts and Spark machine learning models on those Hive tables.

6. We will use Oozie to schedule all of these regular tasks.

Running our first Oozie job

We will start with a very simple example. In this chapter, our use case is to delete a given folder on HDFS via Oozie. In our case study, we get data daily in one folder in HDFS, but we want to delete the previous day's data. We want to keep just latest version in our system. Let's solve our business problem:

1. Log in to Hue and go to **Workflows | Editor**.

2. In the top row of editor, there are various types of actions. Select the Hadoop Fs action.

 Take some time with your mouse over and read the names of various types of actions that Oozie can run.

3. Drag the Hadoop Fs action to the editor as shown in the next screenshot.

4. Give a meaningful name to this action, for example, `my_delete_folder_action`.

5. Give the path of the folder that you want to delete. I have used `/user/`
   `hue/learn_oozie/my_first_oozie_job`. I have also set the name of the
   Workflow as `My First Oozie Job`, as shown in the following screenshot:

Hue Workflow editor

6. Make these changes and click on **Save** for the Workflow.

7. In a separate SSH session, let's create this directory in HDFS using the
   following commands:

```
$ ssh root@127.0.0.1 -p 2222
$ sudo su hue
$ hadoop fs -mkdir -p /user/hue/learn_oozie/my_first_oozie_job
$ hadoop fs -ls /user/hue/learn_oozie
```

8. In the Oozie editor, click on the **Submit** button (similar to the play button on
   a DVD player)

9. Click once more to confirm the submission and wait for your job to finish.
   From the following screenshot, we can see that our first job has been
   completed successfully:

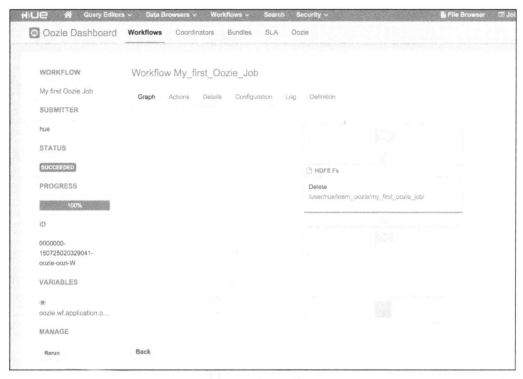

Hue workflow success

10. To confirm that the folder has been really deleted, go to the SSH session and enter the following command:

```
$ hadoop fs -ls /user/hue/learn_oozie
```

11. Come back to the Hue editor where we got confirmation that our job has completed successfully. Click on the **Definition** tab and see the actual code generated by the Hue editor. It should look like the following code:

```
<workflow-app name="My_first_Workflow"
xmlns="uri:oozie:workflow:0.5">
  <start to="fs-2178"/>
    <kill name="Kill">
      <message>Action failed, error
      message[${wf:errorMessage(wf:lastErrorNode())}]</message>
    </kill>
    <action name="fs-2178">
      <fs>
        <delete path='${nameNode}
        /user/hue/learn_oozie/my_first_oozie_job'/>
```

```
    </fs>
    <ok to="End"/>
    <error to="Kill"/>
  </action>
  <end name="End"/>
</workflow-app>
```

Let's take some time to understand this; there are few concepts to pick from here. The code is composed of following:

- Top level declaration that indicates this is Workflow
- Start definition
- Kill definition
- Action definition
- End definition

If you remember, Workflow tells Oozie *what* to do. The *what* part comprises different Oozie actions. We write all our business logic using actions, which can be of various types, for example Pig, MapReduce, Hive, Fs action, and so on. Each Workflow has one start node and one end node. Composition in defined order of nodes make the *what* part of Oozie Workflow.

Now, check the XML code carefully to understand the flow of the code. In this example, our Workflow has the name `My_first_Oozie_Job`. At the `start` tag, we are directing Oozie to go to the action whose name is `my_delete_folder_action`. This action is of type `fs`. This action represents the Hadoop filesystem operations. In our example, we are just telling Oozie to delete the folder we created. We are saying this: if this completes successfully, go to the end (`ok to="End"`); otherwise go to kill on error (`error to="Kill"`).

Take sometime to read all the supported options in Hadoop Fs actions and try to do the same in Oozie via Hue. You can refer to details of Oozie Fs action documentation at `http://oozie.apache.org/docs/4.2.0/WorkflowFunctionalSpec.html#a3.2.4_Fs_HDFS_action`. Try to create Workflow in which you should try to create folder and folder change permissions.

Types of nodes

Workflow is composed of nodes; the logical DAG of nodes represents *what* part of the work is done by Oozie. Each node does a specified work and on success moves to one node or moves to another node on failure. For example, on success it goes to the OK node and on failure it goes to the Kill node.

Nodes in the Oozie Workflow are of the following types:

- Control flow nodes
- Action nodes

Let's discuss them in detail.

Control flow nodes

These nodes are responsible for defining start, end, and control flow of what to do inside the Workflow. These can be one of following:

- Start node
- End node
- Kill node
- Decision node
- Fork and Join node

You have already seen the examples of the Start, End, and Kill nodes. In the context of programming, we can say that Decision nodes represent the switch or if else conditions. Fork and Join nodes represent the parallel branches of code.

Let's see a sample syntax for Decision and Fork/Join nodes next.

Here's the general syntax for a Decision node:

```
<workflow-app name="[workflow_name]"
xmlns="uri:oozie:workflow:0.5">
  ...
  <decision name="[node_name]">
    <switch>
      <case to="[node_name1]">[PREDICATE]</case>
        ...
      <case to="[node_name2]">[PREDICATE]</case>
      <default to="[node_name3]"/>
    </switch>
  </decision>
  ...
</workflow-app>
```

Here's the general syntax for the Fork and Join nodes:

```
<workflow-app name="[workflow_name]"
xmlns="uri:oozie:workflow:0.5">
  ...
  <fork name="[node_name]">
    <path start="[node_name1]" />
    ...
    <path start="[node_name2]" />
  </fork>
  ...
  <join name="[join_node_name]" to="[node_name3" />
  ...
</workflow-app>
```

Action nodes

Action nodes represent the actual processing tasks that are executed when called. These are of various types, for example, Pig action, Hive action, and MapReduce action. We will learn how to use them in course of this book.

> Read the XSD schema of the Workflow at http://oozie.apache.
> org/docs/4.2.0/WorkflowFunctionalSpec.html#Oozie_
> Schema_Version_0.5 to see the XSD of the concepts that we have
> covered so far. Note the elements which are mandatory and which are
> optional in these XML elements. Read about the following complex
> types: complexType name="FS", complexType name="ACTION",
> complexType name="WORKFLOW-APP", complexType
> name="START", and complexType name="END".

Let's finish off this chapter with two more topics that are very useful for checking the progress of the job submitted.

Oozie web console

Oozie web console is a web-based tool that gives a read-only view about the jobs.

In your web browser, open the URL http://127.0.0.1:11000/oozie, as shown in the following screenshot:

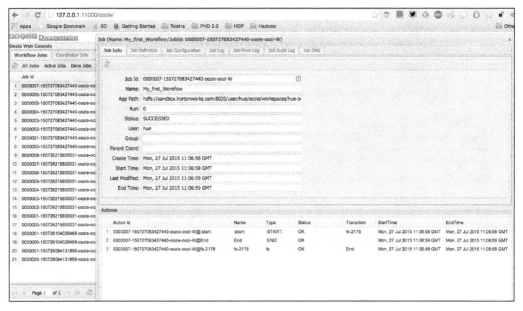

Oozie web console

At the top of the screen, we have following tabs:

- **Workflows**
- **Coordinators**
- **Bundles**
- **System Info**
- **Instrumentation**
- **Settings**

Click on our job ID My First Oozie Job; you can see we have many other jobs also run. You will have a different view. Click on your job and see that Oozie has divided the jobs as per tasks in the Workflow. Start the Fs action and end were the steps for the Workflow, so each of them is represented in the log.

Click on the last tab that says **Job DAG**. This shows the flow of the job. Since our job was simple, DAG is just a linear flow. In future jobs, we will see more complex DAG.

The important use of the console is when our job fails. Let's see an example of a job that has not completed successfully. We can click on the required action to see the logs and detailed error messages as shown in the following screenshot:

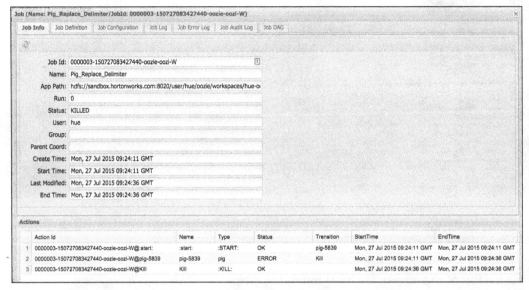

Oozie failed job web console

 If the job is not showing time as per your time zone, use the Oozie web console's **Settings** tab and change the time zone settings as per your time zone.

The Oozie command line

In the last section of this chapter, we will see how to view the status of our job via the command line. We have already seen one way of checking job status via the Oozie web console.

Start a SSH session to the virtual machine and use the following command:

```
$ oozie job -info 0000007-150727083427440-oozie-oozi-W --oozie
http://sandbox.hortonworks.com:11000/oozie
```

The general syntax is as follows:

```
$ oozie job -info <job_id> --oozie <oozie_server_url>
```

The following screenshot shows the output of the preceding command:

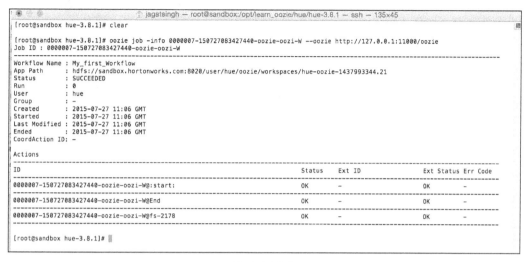

Oozie job info

 Explore the output of the Oozie help job. Note the various options and commands that we can execute on a given job.

Summary

In this chapter, we saw how to run a simple Oozie job from Hue console. We discussed concepts of Workflow in detail and saw how to use Fs action. We also checked the job logs using web console and submitted the job using the command line.

In the next chapter, we will see how to submit a job without using Hue. We will discuss how to use the Oozie command-line tool to submit a job and get an idea about the job.properties file. We will also look at Control nodes, Fork, and Join in detail.

3
Oozie Fundamentals

In this chapter, we will see how to create Oozie Workflow to solve a given business problem. Remember we are learning the *what* part of the data pipeline solution using Workflow in this part of book. We will eventually move to the *when* (time) part using Coordinators in the coming chapters.

In this chapter, we will do the following:

- Create an Oozie Workflow using Hue and by manual XML writing
- Run Oozie applications with and without Hue
- Submit Oozie jobs from command line
- Understand the concept of Control nodes
- Understand Workflow states
- Use expression language functions
- Use the Oozie Email action

Chapter case study

We will start this chapter with a case study example. In the previous chapter, we created our first Oozie Workflow to delete a given directory; we will build on top of that.

In this chapter, our use case is as follows.

On a daily basis we get incoming data in a HDFS directory. Our Workflow comes into action to process it via a simple Pig script. If we find the directory empty, we send a mail to the support team stating we did not get any data today. This is a very common data ingestion pattern in Hadoop for file-based loads.

There are many concepts, which will be introduced by use of this example; I thought to do it this way rather than sharing the concept first and sharing the example later. Using this example, we will cover the following concepts:

- Decision nodes
- Expression language
- Oozie command-line execution

Let's get started. The data ingestion pipeline for our use case can be represented as follows:

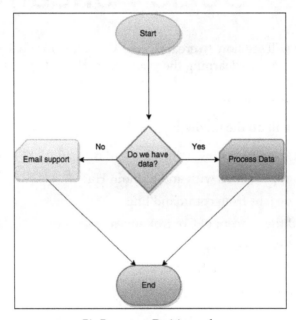

Pig Preprocess Decision node

Open Hue and go to **Editor | Workflows** to create a new Workflow in the Workflow editor. The Start and End nodes are already created by Hue. So, we just need to add three more nodes:

- Decision node
- Email node
- Pig Processing node

If you are not using Hue, then you can move on. Later, when we do the same without Hue, you can pick up and get into action. There is nothing which you cannot do without Hue; it's just that you have to write XML yourself, which is pretty easy. If you want to see the XML, then you can open the ch03 code folder.

We will discuss each of these nodes later after creating the Workflow in Hue. We can see in the flow chart that we have a Decision node that branches depending upon whether the case evaluates to true or false.

Before we even start creating the Workflow, let's see what is inside the Pig script using the following command:

```
cat
<BOOK_CODE_LOCATION>/learn_oozie/ch03/pig/replace_delimiters.pig
```

The Pig script is pretty simple:

```
inputData = load '$inputPath' using PigStorage(',');
store inputData into '$outputPath' using PigStorage('|');
```

It reads the input data, which is comma-separated data, and stores it as pipe-separated data. Perform the following steps:

1. Drag the Pig action in the Hue Workflow editor.

2. Enter the following details:

Field	Value
Script Location	/user/hue/learn_oozie/ch03/pig/replace_ delimiters.pig
Parameters	inputPath=/user/hue/learn_oozie/ch03/input/
Parameters	outputPath=/user/hue/learn_oozie/ch03/output

3. Click on the gear icon on the top-right corner of the Pig action.

4. In the **Prepare** step, add the path to delete:

    /user/hue/learn_oozie/ch03/output

5. This job fails if the output path already exists. So we are just deleting the Pig output path before starting the Pig action.

6. Drag the **Email** action to left of the Pig action in the Hue Workflow editor.

7. Enter the following details:

Field	Value
To addresses	bigdata@mysupport.com.fake
Subject	No data today
Body	No data please check

Note that when you drag two actions side by side, one additional action is automatically inserted by Hue. It says **Fork** action. Click on **Convert to Decision node**, as we need it as Decision node.

8. In the Decision node, we can see the `if` statements, which are case statements of the Decision node. Fill them as shown in following table:

Condition	Transition node
${ fs:dirSize("/user/hue/learn_oozie/ch03/ input") gt 0 }	Pig action
default	Email action

The condition check is syntax and is known as EL functions. It will be discussed in detail shortly.

In simple language, we are saying that if the size of directory data is greater than zero, then call the **Pig** action or else call the **Email** action.

Currently, the Decision nodes cannot be deleted in Hue. If you end up having two, then you have to start over again. So be careful of what you do. It's expected that this will be fixed in Hue 3.9.0. You can read the details at JIRA available at `https://issues. cloudera.org/browse/HUE-2550`. Of course, you can always edit the XML file manually outside Hue.

9. Click on the **Save** button.

   The Workflow should look something like this:

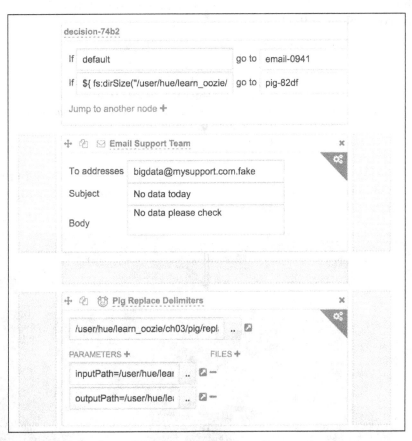

Pig pre-process Workflow editor

10. We are now ready to run our Workflow. But before that, we need to copy the Pig script and create input data for testing. We are copying the book's source code using the following command:

```
hadoop fs -copyFromLocal <BOOK_CODE_LOCATION>/learn_oozie
/user/hue/
```

11. Click on the **Run** button and watch your Workflow running.

12. If the Workflow fails for any reason, click on **Log** to find the error.

13. After the Workflow finishes, click on the **Definition** tab on Hue and check the `workflow.xml` file generated by Hue. I have saved this XML file inside the code folder at the following location:

    `<BOOK_CODE_LOCATION>/learn_oozie/ch03/hue/workflow.xml`

>
> Try to delete the input data folder `/user/hue/learn_oozie/ch03/input` and check whether the Email action is executed or not. You might not get actual e-mail yet, read the *Email action configuration* section on how to configure SMTP server discussed later in this chapter.

14. The `workflow.xml` file, which represents our use case, is shown in the following screenshot. Take some time to read it carefully and compare it with the flowchart we saw earlier:

```xml
1  <workflow-app name="Pig_Replace_Delimiter_Ch03" xmlns="uri:oozie:workflow:0.5">
2      <start to="decision-74b2"/>
3      <kill name="Kill">
4          <message>Action failed, error message[${wf:errorMessage(wf:lastErrorNode())}]</message>
5      </kill>
6      <action name="email-0941">
7          <email xmlns="uri:oozie:email-action:0.1">
8              <to>bigdata@mysupport.com.fake</to>
9              <subject>No data today</subject>
10             <body>No data please check</body>
11         </email>
12         <ok to="End"/>
13         <error to="Kill"/>
14     </action>
15     <decision name="decision-74b2">
16         <switch>
17             <case to="pig-82df">
18                 ${ fs:dirSize(&quot;/user/hue/learn_oozie/ch03/input&quot;) gt 0 }
19             </case>
20             <default to="email-0941"/>
21         </switch>
22     </decision>
23     <action name="pig-82df">
24         <pig>
25             <job-tracker>${jobTracker}</job-tracker>
26             <name-node>${nameNode}</name-node>
27             <prepare>
28                 <delete path="${nameNode}/user/hue/learn_oozie/ch03/output"/>
29             </prepare>
30             <script>/user/hue/learn_oozie/ch03/pig/replace_delimiters.pig</script>
31             <param>inputPath=/user/hue/learn_oozie/ch03/input/</param>
32             <param>outputPath=/user/hue/learn_oozie/ch03/output</param>
33         </pig>
34         <ok to="End"/>
35         <error to="Kill"/>
36     </action>
37     <end name="End"/>
38 </workflow-app>
```

Workflow XML

Our Workflow starts with `decision-74b2` (line 2). Then, Decision node decides where to go, `pig-82df` (line 17 and 23) or `emal-0941` (line 6 and 20). After that, it chooses to `End` or `Kill` depending on whether it is successful or fails. You might notice the names generated by Hue for nodes are not human friendly. You can create your own names when you write `workflow.xml` yourself.

Let's take some time to see each of the sections of Workflow in detail.

The Decision node

The general syntax for the Decision node is as follows:

```
<workflow-app name="[WF-DEF-NAME]" xmlns="uri:oozie:workflow:0.1">
    ...
  <decision name="[NODE-NAME]">
    <switch>
      <case to="[NODE_NAME]">[PREDICATE]</case>
        ...
      <case to="[NODE_NAME]">[PREDICATE]</case>
      <default to="[NODE_NAME]"/>
    </switch>
  </decision>
    ...
</workflow-app>
```

The preceding syntax is the equivalent of `switch` case statements in Java or other languages. There is no fall through of `switch` statements. Depending upon which case statement evaluates to `true`, the corresponding node will be executed. The default case is mandatory for the Decision node.

In our use case, the condition is as follows: if we have any data, then process it, or else drop a mail to the support team"

The default case is to mail the support team.

The Email action

The **Email** action sends an e-mail to `bigdata@mysupport.com.fake` with subject as `No data` and body as `No data please check`.

In a real production job notification, our mail will be more detailed and have context about the failed job, for example, job ID, time, and so on. We will get back to this in a while.

You can also include attachment messages in the mail sent. For details about the Oozie Email action, check the schema on website at `https://oozie.apache.org/docs/4.2.0/DG_EmailActionExtension.html`.

Expression Language functions

Look at line 18 in `workflow.xml`, which says `${ fs:dirSize("/user/hue/learn_oozie/ch03/input") gt 0 }`. This line gives us the size of the HDFS directory. This is an example of the HDFS EL functions.

EL functions allow us to build complex parameterization of the Workflow by providing a predefined set of functions and properties.

There are many types of Expression Language functions:

- Basic EL constants
- Basic EL functions
- Workflow EL functions
- Hadoop EL constants
- Hadoop EL functions
- Hadoop Jobs EL function
- HDFS EL functions
- HCatalog EL functions

We will discuss a few of them in brief.

Basic EL constants

Basic EL constants are representative of the size:

- **KB**: 1 kilobyte
- **MB**: 1 megabyte
- **GB**: 1 gigabyte
- **TB**: 1 terabyte
- **PB**: 1 petabyte

Example usage can be checked if the size of HDFS directory is greater than 5 * GB.

Basic EL functions

Some of the basic EL functions are as follows:

- `String timestamp()`: This gives the current date and time in ISO8601 format
- `String trim(String s)`: This gives the trimmed value of the given string

Workflow EL functions

These are very interesting EL functions. Some of them are:

- `String wf:id()`: Gives the Workflow job ID for the executing Workflow job
- `String wf:name()`: Gives the Workflow application name for the executing Workflow job
- `String wf:lastErrorNode()`: Gives the name of the last Workflow action node that exits with an ERROR exit state
- `String wf:errorMessage(String message)`: Gives the error message for the specified action node.

As an example usage, the preceding functions will be calculated by Oozie depending upon the name of the Workflow (In the current example, `String wf:name()` => `Pig_Replace_Delimiter_Ch03`) and time stamp.

Change the body message of the e-mail message, which we wrote earlier. "We did not get any data for `wf:name()` which executed at `timestamp()`". Try to execute it with no input data now. Notice the change in the e-mail content.

Hadoop EL constants

Following are the EL constants:

- `RECORDS`: This records the counters group name for Hadoop
- `MAP_IN`: This maps the input records counter name
- `MAP_OUT`: This maps the output records counter name
- `REDUCE_IN`: This reduces the input records counter name
- `REDUCE_OUT`: This reduces the output records counter name
- `GROUPS`: 1024 * Hadoop mapper and reducer record groups counter name

HDFS EL functions

We will discuss HDFS EL functions and then move on to a different topic. You can read more about EL functions on Oozie documentation website.

HDFS EL functions are related to the HDFS filesystem. We have already seen one when we checked the size of directory. Some of other functions are as follows:

- `boolean fs:exists(String path)`: Returns `true` or `false` depending on whether the specified path URI exists or not

- `boolean fs:isDir(String path)`: This returns `true` if the specified path URI exists and it is a directory; otherwise, it returns `false`

- `long fs:dirSize(String path)`: This returns the size in bytes of all the files in the specified path

- `long fs:fileSize(String path)`: This returns the size in bytes of a specified file

For all the functions, the path must include the HDFS URI, for example, `hdfs://mycluster:8020/user/hue`.

We will wrap up the section of EL functions here. You can read about all the available EL functions in the online documentation at `https://oozie.apache.org/docs/4.2.0/WorkflowFunctionalSpec.html#a4.2_Expression_Language_Functions`.

Email action configuration

To send e-mails from the Oozie server, we need to configure Oozie with SMTP server details. These settings need to be configured in the `oozie-site.xml` file for the server. The details are as follows:

Parameter	Sample Value
`oozie.email.smtp.host`	`localhost`
`oozie.email.smtp.port`	`25`
`oozie.email.from.address`	`oozie@localhost`
`oozie.email.smtp.auth`	`false`
`oozie.email.smtp.username`	Not needed if auth is `false`
`oozie.email.smtp.password`	Not needed if auth is `false`

Think of some Workflow in which you will do parallel execution of two actions. Try to do the same using Fork and Join action in Hue. In the current example, you can add one more action in which you say you create a flag (Fs touchz) indicating data is received. So add the Fork node before the Pig action and run both Pig and Fs actions together. To do so, you need to drag the Fs action to left of the Pig action.

So far, we have used Hue to do all our work. But there is no need to use Hue to work with Oozie. In this section, we will write `workflow.xml` and learn how to run Oozie jobs from the command line. But before that, we need to learn the following concepts:

- Job property file
- Command-line execution

Job property file

I have written the Workflow with my own convention as per the flowchart we saw at the start. Take some time and compare it with the flowchart. Also, note the use of EL functions, which we saw earlier (replacing `hue` with `wf:user` and e-mail template body section). Check the body message of the `Kill` section in the following screenshot, which is an EL function:

```xml
1  <workflow-app name="Pig_Replace_Delimiter" xmlns="uri:oozie:workflow:0.5">
2
3      <start to="check-data"/>
4
5      <decision name="check-data">
6          <switch>
7              <case to="replace-delimiter">
8                  ${fs:dirSize("/user/hue/learn_oozie/ch03/input") gt 0 }
9              </case>
10             <default to="email-support"/>
11         </switch>
12     </decision>
13
14     <action name="email-support">
15         <email xmlns="uri:oozie:email-action:0.1">
16             <to>bigdata@mysupport.com.fake</to>
17             <subject>No data today</subject>
18             <body>No data for job ${wf:name()} please check. Timestamp ${timestamp()}</body>
19         </email>
20         <ok to="End"/>
21         <error to="Kill"/>
22     </action>
23
24     <action name="replace-delimiter">
25         <pig>
26             <job-tracker>${jobTracker}</job-tracker>
27             <name-node>${nameNode}</name-node>
28             <prepare>
29                 <delete path="${nameNode}/user/${wf:user()}/learn_oozie/ch03/output"/>
30             </prepare>
31             <script>/user/${wf:user()}/learn_oozie/ch03/pig/replace_delimiters.pig</script>
32             <param>inputPath=/user/${wf:user()}/learn_oozie/ch03/input</param>
33             <param>outputPath=/user/${wf:user()}/learn_oozie/ch03/output</param>
34         </pig>
35         <ok to="End"/>
36         <error to="Kill"/>
37     </action>
38
39     <kill name="Kill">
40         <message>Action failed, error message[${wf:errorMessage(wf:lastErrorNode())}]</message>
41     </kill>
42
43     <end name="End"/>
44 </workflow-app>
```

Workflow XML command line

Save the preceding content as `workflow.xml`. In the book source code, it is present in the `<BOOK_CODE_LOCATION>/learn_oozie/ch03/commandline` folder.

If you look at the Workflow carefully, it has the following variables:

- `${jobTracker}`
- `${nameNode}`

When we run a job from the command line, we abstract and provide all these variables in the form of the `job.properties` file as parameters. The `job.properties` file looks like this:

```
# The resource manager RPC port
jobTracker=sandbox.hortonworks.com:8050
# Namenode
nameNode=hdfs://sandbox.hortonworks.com:8020
# Use the Oozie Shared library
oozie.use.system.libpath=True
# Default shared lib path is /user/oozie/share/lib
oozie.libpath=hdfs://sandbox.hortonworks.com:8020/user/oozie/share
/lib
# Read the workflow definition from this path
oozie.wf.application.path=hdfs://sandbox.hortonworks.com:8020/user
/hue/learn_oozie/ch03/commandline
```

The `job.properties` file is a typical Java property file in which you define `key=value` definitions. The values of variables that we used in `workflow.xml` are defined in this property file. Comments in the property file start with a hash (#).

Since we are on the topic of parameters and configuration, we should also discuss a few methods in which we can do the same in Workflows. We will discuss these in detail in future chapters:

- Parameters (inline and command line)
- Global tag `<global>`
- Configurations tag `<configuration>`
- `config-default.xml`

The idea of all of the preceding methods is to avoid code duplication.

Read the XSD schema of Workflow at `http://oozie.apache.org/docs/4.2.0/WorkflowFunctionalSpec.html#Oozie_Schema_Version_0.5` and see the XSD of following concepts which we have covered till now. Note the elements that are mandatory and the ones that are optional in these XML elements. Read about the following complex types: `complexType name="WORKFLOW-APP"`, `complexType name="PARAMETERS"`, and `complexType name="GLOBAL"`.

To see the schema graphically, open the SVG diagram present in `<BOOK_CODE_HOME>/xsd_svg/workflow_0.5.svg` using some modern browser like Chrome. Once opened, click on **Collapse All** and then navigate to the right leaf. Open only the path that you want to check. For example, click on **Collapse All** and then click on the + sign near **Schema**. Then, click on the + sign near **Workflow-app**. You will see something like the following diagram. The goal is to note how the given Workflow element is composed and which of those elements are mandatory or optional:

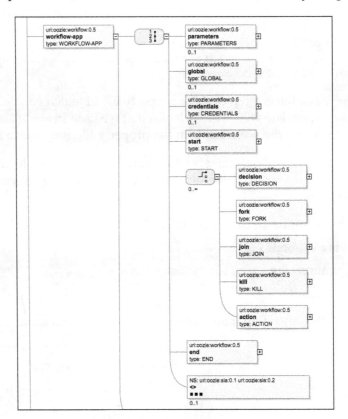

Workflow SVG diagram

Submission from the command line

Following are the steps to submit the job from the command line:

1. Copy the book source code to HDFS if not done at the beginning of this chapter.

2. From the command line, run the job with the following command:

```
cd <BOOK_CODE_LOCATION>/learn_oozie/ch03
oozie job -run -oozie http://localhost:11000/oozie -config
commandline/job.properties
```

3. On successful submission, the command returns the Oozie job ID with which the job was started. We can also monitor the job from Oozie web console with that job ID.

4. Note the job ID returned by the Oozie server and we can use that to check the status of the job from the command line using the following command:

```
oozie job -info <id>
```

5. Wait for the job to finish and then check the output generated in HDFS.

6. Go to Oozie web console at `http://127.0.0.1:11000/oozie/` and see the Job DAG. Does it match with the flowchart which we saw earlier?

 Use the Oozie help job to find the command, which you can use to see the log of the preceding launched job.

 We had one complex job in which Workflow had various Decision nodes, Forks, and Joins. After long tests and trial runs to get the Workflow working, we deployed the code in production. One good thing about using a flowchart is that you can see your data flow and then code. During those days, the Hue editor was not there to see the Workflow visually. The production team deployed the change over late Friday evening and we called the week off. The first thing we did when we came back next week was to check our output. To our surprise, the Workflow never ran. It just was hanging in the PREP state. After checking the code deployment again, we were running out of ideas as to why the job was not running. To our surprise, we found that we never used the flag -run to start the job; we gave the wrong instructions to the production team to just submit the job. One of the tools that comes in handy when troubleshooting a job that is not running (or not running as expected) is the `oozie job log` command.

Workflow states

In this section, we will see all states the Oozie Workflow job goes through when we submit a job. The possible states and transitions are shown in the following figure. The outgoing arrow shows that the job can go from source to destination state:

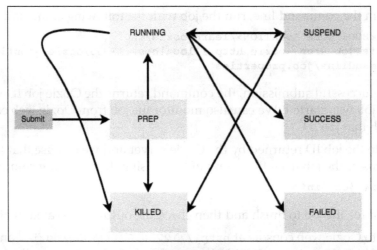

Job states

A Workflow job can be in any of the following states:

- **PREP**: When we initially submit the Workflow to the Oozie server and it's not running, the job is in **PREP** state

- **RUNNING**: When job starts execution, it goes to this state

- **SUSPENDED**: A running job, which is suspended, will be in this state unless the Workflow is resumed

- **SUCCEEDED**: When a **RUNNING** Workflow job completes successfully to the End node, it is said to be **SUCCEEDED**

- **KILLED**: When an administrator kills a **CREATED**, **RUNNING**, or **SUSPENDED** Workflow job or the owner via a request to Oozie, the Workflow job ends and reaches the **KILLED** state

- **FAILED**: When a **RUNNING** Workflow job fails due to an error, it ends and reaches the **FAILED** final state

Summary

In this chapter, we covered a lot of ground. We saw how to write Oozie `workflow.xml` and run it via the Oozie command line. We also discussed how to check the status of the same using command line. Besides this, we covered the concepts of Decision and Fork nodes, EL functions, and Workflow states.

In the next chapter, we will discuss Coordinators that decide the *when* component of data processing pipeline scheduling via Oozie. We will also see how to run MapReduce jobs using Oozie.

4
Running MapReduce Jobs

In this chapter, we will learn how to run MapReduce jobs using Oozie. MapReduce jobs are of two types: Java MapReduce jobs and Streaming jobs. Streaming jobs are written in languages other than Java. We will also enter in to the world of *when* part of Workflow execution using Coordinators to schedule our jobs.

In this chapter, we will do the following:

- Run Java MapReduce jobs from Oozie
- Run Streaming jobs from Oozie
- Run Coordinator jobs

From the concept point of view, we will:

- Understand the concept of Coordinators
- Understand the concept of cron-based frequency schedules
- Understand the importance of timezone in Oozie
- Understand the concept of Datasets

Chapter case study

The customer for whom we work also keeps track of what its competitors are doing. They keep a close eye on all the press releases, job postings, and public interactions of competitors. Information about competitors from various sources is captured in text format and fed to the Hadoop system. Every weekend, analysis is done to see trending topics and words, which are used by competitors to guess about the areas they are working or investing in.

The preceding paragraph is an example of first-level text analytics problem in Big Data space. To solve this problem, we will run classic word count using MapReduce. We will use it for word count each time a given word appears in all of the documents.

Running MapReduce jobs from Oozie

We will see how to write a simple MapReduce job for word count and schedule it via Oozie. Later, we will wrap this in our first Coordinator job. Along this journey, we will learn some concepts and apply them in examples.

I have already saved one word count Java MapReduce code, which we will try to run over our input data. Let's dive into the code. You can check out the `mapreduce` folder in `Book_Code_Folder/learn_oozie/ch04/`.

 Check the `workflow_0.5.xsd` file in the `xsd_svg` folder and note the inputs needed for the MapReduce action to run.

The Workflow is shown in the following code and we can see the arguments are the same as the one we need in the Hadoop `jar` command for running a MapReduce job. At the start of the job, we delete the `output` folder as Hadoop fails the job if the `output` folder already exists.

The mapper that we need is `life.jugnu.learnoozie.ch04.WordCountMapper` and the reducer is `life.jugnu.learnoozie.ch04.WordCountReducer`. Both of them are present in `jar` from the `lib` folder in directory where this `workflow.xml` is. Oozie includes all the files in the `lib` folder to the classpath of a job when it is running over the cluster:

```
<workflow-app name="Mapreduce_Job" xmlns="uri:oozie:workflow:0.5">
  <start to="wordcount"/>
    <kill name="Kill">
      <message>Action failed, error
      message[${wf:errorMessage(wf:lastErrorode())}]</message>
    </kill>
    <action name="wordcount">
      <map-reduce>
        <job-tracker>${jobTracker}</job-tracker>
        <name-node>${nameNode}</name-node>
          <prepare>
            <delete path="${nameNode}/user/hue/learn_oozie/
            ch04/mapreduce/output"/>
          </prepare>
            <configuration>
```

```xml
        <property>
          <name>mapreduce.input.fileinputformat.inputdir</name>
          <value>${input}</value>
        </property>
        <property>
          <name>mapreduce.output.fileoutputformat.outputdir
          </name>
          <value>${output}</value>
        </property>
        <property>
          <name>mapreduce.job.map.class</name>
          <value>life.jugnu.learnoozie.ch04.WordCountMapper
          </value>
        </property>
        <property>
          <name>mapreduce.job.reduce.class</name>
          <value>life.jugnu.learnoozie.ch04.WordCountReducer
          </value>
        </property>
        <property>
          <name>mapred.mapper.new-api</name>
          <value>true</value>
        </property>
        <property>
          <name>mapred.reducer.new-api</name>
          <value>true</value>
        </property>
        <property>
          <name>mapreduce.map.output.key.class</name>
          <value>org.apache.hadoop.io.Text</value>
        </property>
        <property>
          <name>mapreduce.map.output.value.class</name>
          <value>org.apache.hadoop.io.LongWritable</value>
        </property>
      </configuration>
    </map-reduce>
    <ok to="End"/>
    <error to="Kill"/>
  </action>
  <end name="End"/>
</workflow-app>Job properties
```

The job.properties file

The variable values for input and output are being passed from the `job.properties` file. When we discuss the concept of Datasets, we will see how to calculate the input path dynamically from Datasets. In the current example, we are going to use static paths. The `job.properties` file provides all the values for variables declared in Workflow. The corresponding `job.properties` file is shown here:

```
jobTracker=sandbox.hortonworks.com:8050
nameNode=hdfs://sandbox.hortonworks.com:8020
oozie.use.system.libpath=True
oozie.wf.application.path=hdfs://sandbox.hortonworks.com:8020/user
/hue/learn_oozie/ch04/mapreduce
oozie.libpath=hdfs://sandbox.hortonworks.com:8020/user/oozie/share/lib
input=/user/hue/learn_oozie/ch04/mapreduce/input/
output=/user/hue/learn_oozie/ch04/mapreduce/output
```

Running the job

Let's run this job using the following steps:

1. Open an SSH session to the virtual machine running our cluster.
2. Copy the full code of the chapter if not yet done into HDFS.
3. Submit and run the job.
4. Go to the folder where code is present and run the Oozie job using the following command:

    cd <BOOK_CODE_FOLDER>/learn_oozie/ch04/mapreduce

    oozie job -run -oozie http://localhost:11000/oozie -config job.properties

    It will return the job ID and then you can check the status of the running job in Oozie web console.

5. Once the job is complete, you can check the `output` folder placed at `/user/hue/learn_oozie/ch04/mapreduce`.

Running Oozie MapReduce job

Oozie has a command-line functionality to submit a job, which has just a MapReduce action. The command-line option that we saw in the previous action can be used anywhere when we have a Workflow or Coordinator with complex DAG.

To run Oozie job, which is just a simple MapReduce, we can use the command options shown in the following screenshot:

```
                                   1. hue@sandbox:/root (ssh)

   oozie mapreduce <OPTIONS> : submit a mapreduce job
                   -auth <arg>            select authentication type [SIMPLE|KERBEROS]
                   -config <arg>          job configuration file '.properties'
                   -D <property=value>    set/override value for given property
                   -doas <arg>            doAs user, impersonates as the specified user
                   -oozie <arg>           Oozie URL

[hue@sandbox root]$
```

Oozie MapReduce command line

Here's an example:

```
oozie mapreduce -config job.properties -oozie
http://localhost:11000/oozie
```

 We can also choose to pass on variables such as `input` and `output` from the command line.

In this section, we made our Workflow using the MapReduce action and used the command-line Oozie job option with the `job.properties` file to run the same.

Let's move on to the next topic of Coordinators.

Coordinators

Coordinators allow us to run interdependent Workflows as data pipelines based on some starting criteria. They decide the *when* part of execution of Oozie job. Most of the Oozie jobs are triggered at a given scheduled time interval or when input Dataset is present for triggering the job. Here are a few important definitions related to Coordinators:

- **Nominal time**: This the scheduled time at which job should execute. For example, we process press release every day at 8:00 P.M.

- **Actual time**: This is the real time when the job runs. In some cases, if the input data does not arrive, the job might start late. This type of data-dependent job triggering is indicated by the `<done-flag>` tag (more on this later). The `done-flag` gives a signal to start the job execution.

The general skeleton template of Coordinator is shown in the following figure named Coordinator template XML:

```
1   <coordinator>
2       <parameters></parameters>
3       <controls>
4           <timeout></timeout>
5           <concurency></concurency>
6           <execution></execution>
7           <throttle></throttle>
8       </controls>
9       <datasets>
10          <include></include>
11          <dataset></dataset>
12      </datasets>
13      <input-events>
14          <data-in></data-in>
15      </input-events>
16      <output-events>
17          <data-out></data-out>
18      </output-events>
19      <action>
20          <workflow></workflow>
21          <sla></sla>
22      </action>
23  </coordinator>
```

Coordinator template XML

The `<parameters>` tag on line 2 in the preceding screenshot are any variables defined in the Coordinator. Next, let's talk about Datasets.

Datasets

File-based ingestion is a common pattern in Hadoop. Take a simple case of daily input of press release data, which are documented in text format and we store them over night in Hadoop.

Let the sample file be `MyCompetitorPR_2014-08-10.txt`.

It is just a simple file, which is in the `FileName_YYYY-MM-DD.txt` format. Instead of taking input from a simple path like `/user/hue/learn_oozie/ch04/mapreduce/input/` (same path everyday), we would want to take it from path which is dependent on date. For example, each day we consume from the corresponding date folder.

Coming back to our problem space, we are going to push data to a new folder everyday. We will push them to HDFS using the `hadoop fs -copyFromLocal` command.

The file `MyCompetitorPR_2014-08-10.txt` will be pushed to `${nameNode}/learn_oozie/ch04/input/pressrelease/2014/08/10`.

 Lambda architecture recommends the immutable data states. Therefore, we prefer keeping all the input in the Hadoop platform untouched in its original state. This is also called the Golden copy. This gives us an advantage as we can choose to replay some other business logic in case we find any mistake in the old processing logic or it strikes us later down the timeline when we started. You can read more about Lambda architecture at `http://lambda-architecture.net/`.

In terms of Dataset, the press release can be defined as follows:

```
<dataset name="pressrelease" frequency="${coord:days(1)}" initial-
instance="2015-08-15T00:00Z" timezone="Australia/Sydney">
  <uri-template>
    {nameNode}/learn_oozie/ch04/input/pressrelease/
    ${YEAR}/${MONTH}/${DAY}
  </uri-template>
  <done-flag>_SUCCESS</done-flag>
</dataset>
```

A Dataset is a collection of data, which is identified by some logical name. In case of the preceding example, the logical name is resolved by filling the values of the YEAR, MONTH, and DAY variables. The data in Dataset is immutable and produced at regular intervals with defined frequency; in the preceding example, it is one day (`coord:days(1)`). We will see it in detail in the *Frequency and time* section.

Datasets (note plural) is a group of individual datasets. They are defined once in the Hadoop platform and those definitions can be reused among any number of coordinator jobs. For example, we define the Dataset `pressrelease`, specify that it comes once a day, and tell that it can be found with a path represented by `<uri-template>`. In the same way, we can define other Datasets like job postings, public interactions, and so on.

Since the Datasets is a collection of datasets (as shown in the following figure), they can be represented by a collection of individual Datasets and include file representation. We can include something similar to `#include iostream.h` from the C++ world. It is like reusing something that has been already defined somewhere.

As best practice for organizing data inside a cluster, you will represent them as Dataset and store all the logical `datasets.xml` files in one place on HDFS so that all Coordinator jobs can reuse them. Take a look at the following diagram that represents SVG (present in the `xsd_svg` and `coordinator_0.4.xsd` folders):

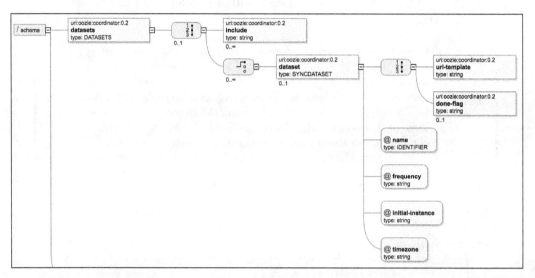

Dataset representation

Dataset definition needs the following details:

Field	Definition	Example
name	Dataset name	pressrelease
frequency	Indicates time in minutes at which data is created and uses EL expressions to represent time	${coord:days(1)}
initial-instance	The UTC date and time of the initial instance of the Dataset	2015-08-15T00:00Z
timezone	The timezone of the Dataset	Australia/Sydney
url-template	The URI template that identifies the Dataset is made up of constants (YEAR) and variables	namenode/learn_oozie/ch04/input/pressrelase/{YEAR}/{MONTH}/{DAY}
done-flag	Indicates when a Dataset instance is ready to be consumed	_SUCCESS file

Frequency and time

Frequency represents how regular the given event is going to happen. It is always represented in minutes. So, we can also say that minimum granularity of Oozie is minutes. The following are prebuilt functions that represent the frequency:

Frequency	Value	Example
`coord:minutes(int n)`	*n* minutes	`coord:minutes(30)` is 30 minutes
`coord:hours(int n)`	*n*60* minutes	`coord:hours(2)` is 120 minutes
`coord:days(int n)`	Variable minutes depending on timezone	`coord:days(3)` is the number of minutes in three days of defined timezone, starting with day of nominal time
`coord:endOfDays(int n)`	Variable minutes depending on timezone	Same as the `coord:days()` function, but it shifts the first occurrence to the end of day for the given timezone before calculating the interval in minutes
`coord:months(int n)`	Variable minutes depending on timezone	`coord:months(2)` is the number of minutes in two months of timezone at the time of calculation, starting with nominal time
`coord:endOfMonths(int n)`	Variable minutes depending on timezone	Same as the `coord:months()` function, but it shifts the first occurrence to the end of the month for the given timezone before calculating the interval in minutes

You can refer to some of the frequency and time examples given in the Oozie documentation at `https://oozie.apache.org/docs/4.2.0/CoordinatorFunctionalSpec.html#a4.4._Frequency_and_Time-Period_Representation`.

Cron syntax for frequency

Oozie has a cron-type syntax for declaring frequency. It is inspired by the Quartz scheduler that can be found at `http://quartz-scheduler.org/api/2.2.1/org/quartz/CronExpression.html`.

Oozie cron description does not allow granularity up to seconds. The general format is as follows:

```
|Minute | Hour | Day of Month | Month | Day of Week|
```

The following table shows the fields and values:

Field Name	Allowed Values	Allowed Special Characters
Minutes	0-59	, - * /
Hours	0-23	, - * /
Day-of-Month	1-31	, - * ? / L W
Month	1-12 or JAN-DEC	, - * /
Day-of-Week	1-7 or SUN-SAT	, - * ? / L #
Year (Optional)	empty, 1970-2199	, - * /

Let's take some time to read about these special characters:

- The asterisk (*) specifies all values. For example, * in the hour field means every hour.

- The question mark (?) is allowed for the Day-of-Month and Day-of-Week fields. It specifies no specific value.

- The hyphen (-) is used to depict range of values. Let's say we want to run a job from 9:00 A.M. to 12:00 P.M., we can specify it as 9-12 in the Hours field.

- The comma (,) is used to indicate list of values. When we want to run a job for the month of January, February, and March, we can specify it as JAN, FEB, MAR in the Month field.

- The / character is used to specify initial value and increments. For example, when we want to start at 5 minutes and do something with an interval of 15 minutes, we can specify something like 0/15 in the Minutes field.

- The letter L is allowed for the Day-of-Month and Day-of-Week fields. This says that we want last value for day of month or day of week where it is used. For example, L in the month field means 31 for January, 28 for February, and so on. L in the Day of Week field means 7 or Saturday. It can also used in conjugation with another value in the Day-of-Week field, for example 6L means the last Friday of the month.

- The letter W can be used in the Day-of-Month field. It indicates the weekday (Monday to Friday) nearest to given day. For example, we want to run a job on some working weekday nearest to 15th, so we specify 15W as the value for the Day-of-Month field. If 15th is a Saturday, the trigger will fire on Friday (14). If 15th is a Sunday, the trigger will fire on Monday (16). If 15th is a Tuesday, then it will fire on Tuesday the 15th.

- The letters L and W can also be used together for the Day-of-Month field to give LW, which means that this job will run on last weekday of the month.

- The # character can be used for the Day-of-Week field. For example, when we want to run some job on third Friday of the month, we can specify it as 6#3.

The legal characters and the names of months and days of the week are not case sensitive.

The following table shows the examples of these characters:

Cron Expression	Meaning
10 9 * * *	Runs every day at 9:10 A.M., * means every
10,30,45 10 * *	Runs every day at 10:10 A.M., 10:30 A.M., and 10:45 A.M. (comma means combination)
1 2 L-3 * *	Runs every third-to-last day of the month at 2:01 A.M.
1 2 6W 3 ?	Runs on the nearest weekday to March 6 every year at 2:01 A.M.
10 3 * 4 4#2	Runs every second Wednesday of April at 3:10 A.M. every year
0 12,13 * * MON-FRI	Runs every weekday at 12 P.M. and 1 P.M.

Timezone

The timezone indicates the timezone in which the calculation of nominal time should be carried out. The default Oozie processing timezone is UTC. If you remember, the frequency calculations are based on minutes. So depending upon the timezone you are in, the minutes of the day can be different when daylight saving is effective. As a golden rule, if you are in an area where daylight savings are used, then just see the timezone and use it in the value for timezone. A good reference is to see the TZ reference that can be found at `https://en.wikipedia.org/wiki/List_of_tz_` `database_time_zones`.

Cron frequency expression uses the Oozie server processing timezone. Since the default Oozie processing timezone is UTC, we need to change our cron expression with the correct time as per UTC. For example, the time 04:45 A.M. in UTC is same as 2:45 P.M. in the Australia/Sydney timezone. So the cron expression would be `45 4 * * *`. See the example of Coordinator v1 in the upcoming section.

I came from India to work in Australia. India is vast in size but compared to Australia, it is very small. In India, we have one timezone for the entire nation. However, in Australia we have different timezone and few places change there time during daylight savings (`https://en.wikipedia.org/wiki/Daylight_` `saving_time`). It was my first daylight saving experience and watching the clock go back one hour is a different experience (at least for first timers like me). It also gives one hour extra sleep!

In Oozie, we had coded our jobs with static time and after the time shifted, we had issues to keep the jobs run at required timings. For example, the job was coded to run at 4:00 P.M. everyday (by default, all timezone in Oozie are UTC) but our jobs were off by one hour with the change in time. We had to change our jobs and submit with the correct timezone. This made our job conform to both forward and reverse time flow. It is important to choose the correct timezone if your place has daylight savings. You can configure timezone in the Oozie by setting the timezone for Oozie jobs. See the list of timezone by using the command `oozie info -time zones` and pick the one that matches yours.

The <done-flag> tag

The <done flag> tag indicates when a dataset instance is ready to be processed. Here are the various options for <done flag>:

- If the <done-flag> tag is not present, the Coordinator will not start till the file named _SUCCESS is present in the directory. In our file-based load use case the process that is copying the files to HDFS will also create the _SUCCESS flag using the hadoop fs -touchz command.

- If the <done-flag> tag is there but the tag is empty as <done-flag></done-flag>, then the directory (if present) gives a signal to the Coordinator that the Dataset is ready.

- If the <done-flag> tag is there but has some filename, Oozie will check for the presence of the file with given name in the tag in the directory, for example, if the filename is <done-flag>_DATA_LOAD_DONE</done-flag>, Oozie will check the existence of the file _DATA_LOAD_DONE.

Initial instance

Initial instance gives the first value of the Dataset, which can be found in HDFS.

My first Coordinator

In this section, we will write the scheduled job for running out the MapReduce Workflow. Let's start with a simple Coordinator declaration. The code for the following example is present in the folder BOOK_CODE_HOME/learn_oozie/ch04/mapreduce_coordinator/v1.

Coordinator v1 definition

The Coordinator definition present in the coordinator.xml is as follows:

```xml
<coordinator-app name="My_First_Coordinator"
frequency="${frequency}" start="${start_date}" end="${end_date}"
timezone="Australia/Sydney" xmlns="uri:oozie:coordinator:0.4">
  <action>
    <workflow>
      <app-path>${wf_application_path}</app-path>
    </workflow>
  </action>
</coordinator-app>
```

The Coordinator definition is simple. It says, "Run the Workflow `wf_application_path` with the given arguments `start_date`, `end_date`, and `frequency`."

job.properties v1 definition

Look at the values for variables declared in `workflow.xml`. We will define them in the `job.properties` file:

```
# Time and schedule details
start_date=2015-08-14T22:58Z
end_date=2015-08-25T22:58Z
frequency=48 4 * * *
# Cluster and Oozie setup details
jobTracker=sandbox.hortonworks.com:8050
nameNode=hdfs://sandbox.hortonworks.com:8020
oozie.use.system.libpath=True
oozie.libpath=hdfs://sandbox.hortonworks.com:8020/user/oozie/share
/lib
# Workflow to run
wf_application_path=hdfs://sandbox.hortonworks.com:8020/user/hue/
learn_oozie/ch04/mapreduce
# Coordinator to run
oozie.coord.application.path=hdfs://sandbox.hortonworks.com:8020/
user/hue/learn_oozie/ch04/mapreduce_coordinator/v1
# Parameters for workflow
input=/user/hue/learn_oozie/ch04/mapreduce/input/
output=/user/hue/learn_oozie/ch04/mapreduce/output
```

Go to the `v1` folder using the following command:

```
cd BOOK_CODE_HOME/learn_oozie/ch04/mapreduce_coordinator/v1
```

Copy the following code to HDFS if not already done at start of the book:

```
hadoop fs -copyFromLocal BOOK_CODE_HOME/learn_oozie/ch04
/user/hue/learn_oozie
```

```
# Run the coordinator
```

```
oozie job -run -config job.properties -oozie
http://localhost:11000/oozie
```

Let's understand the `job.properties` file.

We are running the same MapReduce word count Workflow which we wrote earlier. We are saying that the Coordinator has `start_date=2015-08-14T22:58Z`, `end_date=2015-08-25T22:58Z`, and `frequency=48 4 * * *`. `frequency` says the Workflow should run every day at 04:48 A.M. GMT. Remember that cron frequency expression uses the Oozie server processing timezone by default which is UTC.

In the property file, we are also saying that the Workflow is present at `wf_application_path` and the Coordinator is present at `oozie.coord.application.path`.

To see it in action yourself, you need to edit `start_date end_date` and `frequency` to run it as per time when you are reading the book.

If you note the input and output paths in the property file, they are hardcoded to static values. But our `pressrelease` use case says we will have new data daily added to the cluster and the input path will change. For example, the input path `${nameNode}/learn_oozie/ch04/input/pressrelease/2014/08/10` will change to the output path `${nameNode}/learn_oozie/ch04/output/pressrelease/2014/08/10`.

So, we will revise our code to use the concept of Datasets.

Coordinator v2 definition

In the following definition, I have defined the Datasets in an XML file placed at `BOOK_CODE_HOME/learn_oozie/ch04/datasets/datasets.xml`.

We defined the two Datasets here, `pressrelease` and `wordcount`. We will use `pressrelease` as the input Dataset and `wordcount` as the output Dataset. Note that Dataset definition is similar for both and does not change if it is used as input source or output sink.

In the `frequency` definition, we are saying `coord:days(1)`, which means the Dataset will be generated each day. As per our use case condition, we are getting the `pressrelease` input daily. Further, we have also declared `<done-flag>` as `_SUCCESS`. So the script that is going to copy data to HDFS will also create `<done flag>` using the `hadoop fs -touchz` command.

For example, the filename `MyCompetitorPR_2014-08-10.txt` will be pushed to `${nameNode}/user/hue/learn_oozie/ch04/input/pressrelease/2014/08/10` folder and `<done-flag>` will also be created using the command `hadoop fs -touchz${nameNode}/user/hue/learn_oozie/ch04/input/pressrelease/2014/08/10/_SUCCESS`.

The initial instance says that data history will be present from this day.

Similarly, we have defined the output Dataset as `wordcount`, where output will be stored by the Workflow. The complete `datasets.xml` file is as follows:

```
<datasets>
  <dataset name="pressrelease" frequency="${coord:days(1)}"
    initial-instance="2015-08-15T00:00Z" timezone="Australia/Sydney">
```

```
    <uri-template>${nameNode}/user/hue/learn_oozie/
    ch04/input/pressrelease/${YEAR}/${MONTH}/${DAY}</uri-template>
    <done-flag>_SUCCESS</done-flag>
  </dataset>
  <dataset name="wordcount" frequency="${coord:days(1)}" initial-
  instance="2015-08-15T00:00Z" timezone="Australia/Sydney">
    <uri-template>${nameNode}/user/hue/learn_oozie/ch04/
    output/wordcount/${YEAR}/${MONTH}/${DAY}</uri-template>
    <done-flag>_SUCCESS</done-flag>
  </dataset>
</datasets>
```

Let's revise the `coordinator.xml` file to use the Dataset definition. See the following code snippet for the Coordinator named Coordinator v2:

```
1  <coordinator-app name="My_First_Coordinator_v2" frequency="${frequency}"
2                   start="${start_date}" end="${end_date}" timezone="Australia/Sydney"
3                   xmlns="uri:oozie:coordinator:0.4">
4    <datasets>
5        <include>${data_definitions}</include>
6    </datasets>
7    <input-events>
8      <data-in name="wf_input" dataset="pressrelease">
9        <instance>${coord:current(0)}</instance>
10     </data-in>
11   </input-events>
12   <output-events>
13     <data-out name="wf_output" dataset="wordcount">
14       <instance>${coord:current(0)}</instance>
15     </data-out>
16   </output-events>
17   <action>
18     <workflow>
19       <app-path>${wf_application_path}</app-path>
20       <configuration>
21         <property>
22           <name>input</name>
23           <value>${coord:dataIn('wf_input')}</value>
24         </property>
25         <property>
26           <name>output</name>
27           <value>${coord:dataOut('wf_output')}</value>
28         </property>
29       </configuration>
30     </workflow>
31   </action>
32 </coordinator-app>
33
```

Coordinator v2

Here's the explanation of the code in the preceding screenshot:

- In line 4, we are telling it to use the `datasets.xml` file that we created earlier.

- In line 7, we are asking it to use `pressrelease` as input Dataset for Workflow, by linking it at line 22 with the input variable.

- In lines 9 and 14, we are using the EL functions to calculate which instance of datasets to use as input for the Workflow. We will discuss this in detail in the next chapter. In short, this will calculate the current instance and give it as input for the Workflow.

- In line 13, we are saying it to store output in the `wordcount` Dataset by linking it at line 26 with output variable of Workflow.

The current input resolves to `${nameNode}/user/hue/learn_oozie/ch04/input/pressrelease/2015/08/15` and output resolves to `${nameNode}/user/hue/learn_oozie/ch04/output/wordcount/2015/08/15`. Do not worry if the function `coord:current()` is not clear to you; we will cover all of them in the next chapter.

To use the updated Coordinator, let's revise the `job.properties` file.

job.properties v2 definition

The `job.properties` file is shown in the following example. There is one change from the previous one. We have removed the input and output variables and defined the `datasets.xml` path as variables. From this path, the XML file is picked and all the variables are automatically calculated inside `coordinator.xml` based on the definitions we gave in `datasets.xml`:

```
# Time and schedule details
start_date=2015-08-14T22:58Z
end_date=2015-08-25T22:58Z
frequency=5 6 * * *
# Cluster and Oozie setup details
jobTracker=sandbox.hortonworks.com:8050
nameNode=hdfs://sandbox.hortonworks.com:8020
oozie.use.system.libpath=True
oozie.libpath=hdfs://sandbox.hortonworks.com:8020/user/oozie/share/lib
# Workflow to run
wf_application_path=hdfs://sandbox.hortonworks.com:8020/user/hue/
learn_oozie/ch04/mapreduce
# Coordinator to run
oozie.coord.application.path=hdfs://sandbox.hortonworks.com:8020/user
/hue/learn_oozie/ch04/mapreduce_coordinator/v2
# Datasets
data_definitions=hdfs://sandbox.hortonworks.com:8020/user/hue/
learn_oozie/ch04/datasets/datasets.xml
```

Submit the Oozie job using the `oozie job -run` command and check the Oozie web console to see the status of your job.

Checking the job log

To check Oozie job logs, you can use the following command:

```
oozie job -log 0000005-150815030033629-oozie-oozi-C -oozie
http://localhost:11000/oozie
```

A sample output of this command is as follows:

```
2015-08-15 06:05:51,193  INFO CoordActionInputCheckXCommand:520 -
SERVER[sandbox.hortonworks.com] USER[-] GROUP[-] TOKEN[-] APP[-]
JOB[0000005-150815030033629-oozie-oozi-C] ACTION[0000005-
150815030033629-oozie-oozi-C@1] [0000005-150815030033629-oozie-
oozi-C@1]::ActionInputCheck:: In checkListOfPaths:
hdfs://sandbox.hortonworks.com:8020/learn_oozie/ch04/input/
pressrelease/2015/08/15/_SUCCESS is Missing.
```

Running a MapReduce streaming job

In this section we will learn how to run Hadoop Streaming jobs using Oozie. Hadoop Streaming gives the functionality to use different languages such as Python, C++, and Ruby to write MapReduce code.

> Read the Oozie documentation at `https://oozie.apache.org/docs/4.2.0/WorkflowFunctionalSpec.html#a3.2.2_Map-Reduce_Action` and write a Workflow to run a Streaming job. Schedule the same using Coordinator. You can refer to the sample Python mapper and reducer code available at `http://www.michael-noll.com/tutorials/writing-an-hadoop-mapreduce-program-in-python/`.
>
> Save the Python code from the preceding web links as `mapper.py` and `reducer.py` in the `streaming` folder.

The `<mapper>` tag makes our mapper and reducer file available to Oozie.

The Workflow looks like this:

```
<workflow-app name="Mapreduce_Streaming_example"
xmlns="uri:oozie:workflow:0.5">
  <start to="streaming-c097"/>
    <kill name="Kill">
```

```
      <message>Action failed, error
       message[${wf:errorMessage(wf:lastErrorNode())}]</message>
    </kill>
    <action name="streaming-c097">
      <map-reduce>
        <job-tracker>${jobTracker}</job-tracker>
        <name-node>${nameNode}</name-node>
          <streaming>
            <mapper>mapper.py</mapper>
            <reducer>reducer.py</reducer>
          </streaming>
          <configuration>
            <property>
              <name>mapreduce.input.fileinputformat.inputdir</name>
              <value>/user/hue/learn_oozie/ch04/mapreduce/input/
              </value>
            </property>
            <property>
              <name>mapreduce.output.fileoutputformat.outputdir</name>
              <value>/user/hue/learn_oozie/ch04/streaming/output
              </value>
            </property>
          </configuration>
          <file>/user/hue/learn_oozie/ch04/streaming/mapper.py#
           mapper.py</file>
          <file>/user/hue/learn_oozie/ch04/streaming/reducer.py#
           reducer.py</file>
      </map-reduce>
    <ok to="End"/>
    <error to="Kill"/>
    </action>
  <end name="End"/>
</workflow-app>
```

Summary

In this chapter, we saw how to run Java MapReduce jobs as part of the Oozie Workflow. We discussed the concept of Coordinators and scheduled the job using the same. We also covered datasets, frequency specification, and cron-based schedules.

In the next chapter, we will see how to run Hive jobs from Oozie. We will continue to build our Coordinator concepts.

5
Running Pig Jobs

In this chapter, we will see how to run Pig jobs from Oozie. Pig is a general-purpose data flow language, which makes running and doing ETL on Hadoop very easy. If you are new to Pig, then I suggest you to check out the tutorial on the Pig website (`http://pig.apache.org/docs`).

In this chapter, we will:

- Create Oozie Workflows for Pig actions
- Run Pig jobs from Coordinators

From the concept point of view, we will:

- Understand the concept of parameterization of Dataset instances
- Understand the concept of Coordinator controls
- Understand the concept of `config-defaut.xml`

Chapter case study

We are working on a project related to climate as part of research. So we want to know the rainfall pattern near the Melbourne airport. We want to find out the maximum rainfall that was received in each month. To do this, we will write some Pig code to help analyze the rainfall data for us. We will download the data from `http://www.bom.gov.au/`.

We have already seen how to run Pig action in *Chapter 3, Oozie Fundamentals*, when we replaced delimiters using that. We will continue from those skill levels. We will also discuss the Oozie Pig command-line option to run our job.

The Pig command line

The Pig command for running command-line options is shown in the following screenshot:

```
[root@sandbox ~]# oozie help pig
usage:
        the env variable 'OOZIE_URL' is used as default value for the '-oozie' option
        the env variable 'OOZIE_TIMEZONE' is used as default value for the '-timezone' option
        the env variable 'OOZIE_AUTH' is used as default value for the '-auth' option
        custom headers for Oozie web services can be specified using '-Dheader:NAME=VALUE'

        oozie pig <OPTIONS> -X <ARGS> : submit a pig job, everything after '-X' are pass-through
parameters to pig, any '-D' arguments after '-X' are put in <configuration>
                -auth <arg>             select authentication type [SIMPLE|KERBEROS]
                -config <arg>           job configuration file '.properties'
                -D <property=value>     set/override value for given property
                -doas <arg>             doAs user, impersonates as the specified user
                -file <arg>             pig script
                -oozie <arg>            Oozie URL
                -P <property=value>     set parameters for script
```

Oozie Pig command line

To run the same Pig Oozie script that we used in *Chapter 3*, *Oozie Fundamentals*, use the following command:

```
oozie pig -file
<BOOK_CODE_HOME>/learn_oozie/ch03/pig/replace_delimiters.pig -
oozie http://localhost:11000/oozie -P

inputPath=/user/hue/learn_oozie/ch03/input/ -P

outputPath=/user/hue/learn_oozie/ch05/pig_commandline/output -
config job.properties
```

The path for `-file` is a local path from where the command is being submitted, not HDFS. The job we submit runs as soon as it is submitted.

All the JAR files and other files needed by the Pig job needs to be uploaded onto HDFS under `libpath` beforehand.

The `job.properties` file has following definitions:

```
# job.properties file
jobTracker=sandbox.hortonworks.com:8050
nameNode=hdfs://sandbox.hortonworks.com:8020
oozie.use.system.libpath=True
oozie.libpath=hdfs://sandbox.hortonworks.com:8020/user/oozie/share
/lib
```

To see the XML Workflow file that is generated by Oozie, we can use the following command with the job ID shown at start of the command. The job ID reported to you will be different from the one which I got, so please change it:

oozie job -definition   0000003-150816053813068-oozie-oozi-W

Here's the output:

```
use 'help [sub-command]' for help details
[root@sandbox pig_commandline]# oozie job -definition  0000003-150816053813068-oozie-oozi-W
<workflow-app xmlns="uri:oozie:workflow:0.2" name="oozie-pig">
  <start to="pig1" />
  <action name="pig1">
    <pig>
      <job-tracker>sandbox.hortonworks.com:8050</job-tracker>
      <name-node>hdfs://sandbox.hortonworks.com:8020</name-node>
      <script>dummy.pig</script>
      <param>outputPath=/user/hue/learn_oozie/ch05/pig_commandline/output</param>
      <param>inputPath=/user/hue/learn_oozie/ch03/input/</param>
    </pig>
    <ok to="end" />
    <error to="fail" />
  </action>
  <kill name="fail">
    <message>pig failed, error message[${wf:errorMessage(wf:lastErrorNode())}]</message>
  </kill>
  <end name="end" />
</workflow-app>
[root@sandbox pig_commandline]#
```

Pig job definition

The config-default.xml file

So far, we have done lots of code duplication. We copied the same properties again and again in the property files. Oozie has a concept of `config-default.xml`, which can be used to store such properties. This file is present in the folder where `workflow.xml` is present, and it is automatically parsed for properties. From now onwards, we will use the `config-default.xml` file for all the properties that are common. This file is optional but highly recommended to avoid code duplication. Anything that is common to all Workflows, for example, cluster details, should be added to `config-default.xml`:

```
# default-config.xml
<configuration>
  <property>
    <name>oozie.use.system.libpath</name>
    <value>True</value>
  </property>
  <property>
    <name>oozie.libpath</name>
    <value>hdfs://sandbox.hortonworks.com:8020/user/oozie/share/lib
    </value>
  </property>
  <property>
    <name>fs.defaultFS</name>
    <value>hdfs://sandbox.hortonworks.com:8020</value>
  </property>
  <property>
    <name>nameNode</name>
    <value>hdfs://sandbox.hortonworks.com:8020</value>
  </property>
  <property>
    <name>jobTracker</name>
    <value>sandbox.hortonworks.com:8050</value>
  </property>
  <property>
    <name>mapreduce.jobtracker.address</name>
    <value>sandbox.hortonworks.com:8050</value>
  </property>
</configuration>
```

Pig action

Let's see the Pig script that will help us calculate the maximum rainfall in each month.

I have saved the input data for this chapter in the `input` folder placed at BOOK_CODE_
HOME/learn_oozie/ch05.

If you have already copied the source code for this folder on HDFS at the start of chapter, then it will automatically go to the right place inside HDFS. If not, you can copy the code to HDFS now.

The input data is comma separated and the columns in the data are as follows:

- Product code
- Bureau of Meteorology station number
- Year, Month, Day
- Rainfall amount (millimeter's)
- Period over which rainfall was measured (days)
- Quality

We will write the Pig script and load the raw input data, which is grouped by year and month. Then, we will calculate maximum rainfall for each month.

The following Pig script is present at the path BOOK_CODE_HOME/learn_oozie/ch05/
rainfall/pig:

```
# Pig Script to find Max rain in given month
A = load '${pig_input}' using PigStorage(',') as (product_
code:chararray,station_number:long,year:int,month:int,
day:int,rainfall_in_mm:float,period_in_days:int,
quality:chararray);
B = GROUP A BY (year,month);
C = foreach B generate flatten(group),MAX(A.rainfall_in_mm);
STORE C into '${pig_output}' using PigStorage(',');
```

To see the Pig action XSD specification, go to the `xsd_svg` folder, open the `workflow_0.5.svg` file, and browse to the Pig action. Similar to the MapReduce action and Streaming job, we have file and archive elements that allow us to pass external jars or file's information to Pig action, as shown in the following screenshot:

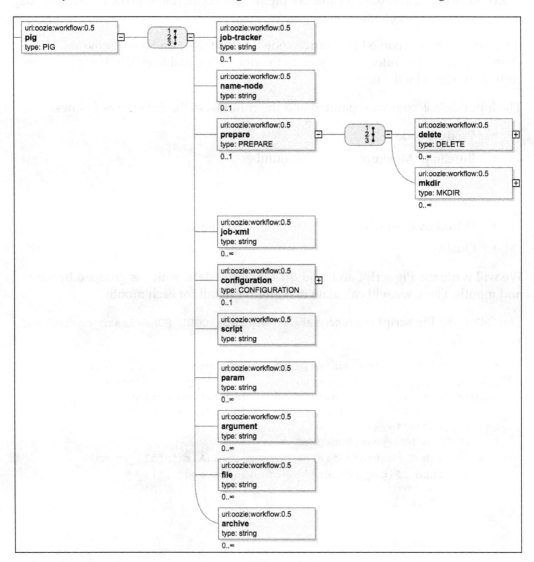

Pig action XSD specification

 In our Pig script, we are not using external jars or UDFs. However, if you need them, you can add that as external jars (more on this in the next chapter).

Now, let's look at the Workflow shown in the following screenshot to know the maximum rainfall in each month.

We are showing the script that should run in line 12, and specifying the input and output parameters in lines 13 and 14:

```
 1  <workflow-app name="max_rainfall" xmlns="uri:oozie:workflow:0.5">
 2
 3      <start to="max_rainfall"/>
 4
 5      <action name="max_rainfall">
 6          <pig>
 7              <job-tracker>${jobTracker}</job-tracker>
 8              <name-node>${nameNode}</name-node>
 9              <prepare>
10                  <delete path="${output}"/>
11              </prepare>
12              <script>/user/hue/learn_oozie/ch05/rainfall/pig/max_rain.pig</script>
13              <param>pig_input=${input}</param>
14              <param>pig_output=${output}</param>
15          </pig>
16          <ok to="End"/>
17          <error to="Kill"/>
18      </action>
19
20      <kill name="Kill">
21          <message>Action failed, error message[${wf:errorMessage(wf:lastErrorNode())}]</message>
22      </kill>
23
24      <end name="End"/>
25  </workflow-app>
```

Pig Workflow v1

The code for this section is available at BOOK_CODE_HOME/learn_oozie/ch05/ rainfall/v1.

Take some time and compare it with the XSD diagram for Pig action.

In our Pig script we do not need any third-party jar or library. If it's needed, we have following choices to pass it on:

- Store it in oozie.libpath
- Store it in the lib folder at the same place where the Workflow is present
- Pass the archive information as a part of the Workflow

The job.properties file is needed for the last part of running the job:

```
# Job Properties file
# Workflow to run
oozie.wf.application.path=hdfs://sandbox.hortonworks.com:8020/user
/hue/learn_oozie/ch05/rainfall/v1
# Parameters for workflow
```

```
input=/user/hue/learn_oozie/ch05/input/
output=/user/hue/learn_oozie/ch05/output/rainfall_pig_workflow
```

Note that we have removed all the repeated properties from the `job.properties` file. All of them have been moved to `config-default.xml` to avoid code duplication. As part of build and packaging, the best practice would be to keep it at one place and then provide them to individual applications of Oozie. We will cover packaging of Oozie code later in this book.

Now, we are ready to execute our job. This will start the processing and find maximum temperature for each month.

Run the Workflow by using the `-run` command of the Oozie job:

oozie job -run -config job.properties

After the completion of the job, you can see the output using the following command:

**hadoop fs -cat
/user/hue/learn_oozie/ch05/output/rainfall_pig_workflow/part-r-00000**

The following screenshot shows the output:

```
[root@sandbox v1]# hadoop fs -cat /user/hue/learn_oozie/ch05/output/rainfall_pig_workflow/part-r-00000
2015,1,11.0
2015,2,21.4
2015,3,16.8
2015,4,10.2
2015,5,5.6
2015,6,6.8
2015,7,27.2
[root@sandbox v1]#
```

Pig output Workflow v1

This concludes our first section, in which we ran a Pig action using Workflow. We also discussed the concept of `config-default.xml` to avoid code duplication and reusing the property values.

In the next section, we will look to schedule our workflow using a Coordinator to produce maximum rainfall collections at end of each month.

Pig Coordinator job v2

We will improve our Coordinator using the concept of Datasets. The code for this section is available at BOOK_CODE_HOME/learn_oozie/ch05/rainfall/v2.

The goal of this section is very simple. We need to learn which dataset instance should be used for processing using the Coordinator dataset parameterization function. We will see them shortly.

The Coordinator for our problem statement is shown in the upcoming screenshot. We are using the Dataset by declaring the definition in line 5 of the screenshot. The corresponding Dataset is defined in the `datasets.xml` file, as shown in the following code:

```
<datasets>
  <dataset name="rainfall" frequency="${coord:months(1)}" initial-
  instance="2015-01-01T00:00Z" timezone="Australia/Sydney">
    <uri-template>
      ${nameNode}/user/hue/learn_oozie/ch05/input/rainfall/${YEAR}/
      ${MONTH}/
    </uri-template>
    <done-flag>_SUCCESS</done-flag>
  </dataset>
  <dataset name="max_rainfall" frequency="${coord:months(1)}"
  initial-instance="2015-01-01T00:00Z" timezone="Australia/Sydney">
    <uri-template>
      ${nameNode}/user/hue/learn_oozie/ch05/processed/max_rainfall/
      ${YEAR}/${MONTH}/
    </uri-template>
    <done-flag>_SUCCESS</done-flag>
  </dataset>
</datasets>
```

Since we have a monthly frequency, the first instance for rainfall will resolve to path `/user/hue/learn_oozie/ch05/input/rainfall/2015/01`, the second one to `/user/hue/learn_oozie/ch05/input/rainfall/2015/02`, and so on. It is same for the `max_rainfall` Dataset as well.

Let's come back to `coordinator.xml`, which is shown in the following screenshot. In `input-events` on line 8, we are saying take `rainfall` as input. In `output-events` on line 13, we are saying give `max_rainfall` as output.

Note the element in both input and output events. We have defined the EL function, which says current(0):

```
 1  <coordinator-app name="max_rainfall_scheduler_v1" frequency="${frequency}"
 2                  start="${start_date}" end="${end_date}" timezone="Australia/Sydney"
 3                  xmlns="uri:oozie:coordinator:0.4">
 4      <datasets>
 5          <include>${data_definitions}</include>
 6      </datasets>
 7      <input-events>
 8        <data-in name="wf_input" dataset="rainfall">
 9          <instance>${coord:current(0)}</instance>
10        </data-in>
11      </input-events>
12      <output-events>
13        <data-out name="wf_output" dataset="max_rainfall">
14          <instance>${coord:current(0)}</instance>
15        </data-out>
16      </output-events>
17      <action>
18        <workflow>
19          <app-path>${wf_application_path}</app-path>
20          <configuration>
21            <property>
22              <name>input</name>
23              <value>${coord:dataIn('wf_input')}</value>
24            </property>
25            <property>
26              <name>output</name>
27              <value>${coord:dataOut('wf_output')}</value>
28            </property>
29          </configuration>
30        </workflow>
31      </action>
32  </coordinator-app>
```

Coordinator v1 rainfall

Take some time to read coordinator.xml again; it is very important to understand all the concepts used in the example.

The property file for this Coordinator is defined as follows. Note the backdated start date and frequency. We are saying it to repeat the job on the last day of each month (L) at 23:55 hours:

```
# Time and schedule details
start_date=2015-01-01T00:00Z
end_date=2015-12-31T00:00Z
frequency=55 23 L * ?
nameNode=hdfs://sandbox.hortonworks.com:8020
# Workflow to run
wf_application_path=hdfs://sandbox.hortonworks.com:8020/user/hue/
learn_oozie/ch05/rainfall/v2
```

```
# Coordinator to run
oozie.coord.application.path=hdfs://sandbox.hortonworks.com:8020/
user/hue/learn_oozie/ch05/rainfall/v2
# Datasets
data_definitions=hdfs://sandbox.hortonworks.com:8020/user/hue/
learn_oozie/ch05/rainfall/datasets/datasets.xml
```

If not done yet, then let's copy the code from the book to HDFS.

Trigger the job using the following command:

`oozie job -run job.properties`

Wait for some time for the job to start. The job starts its first instance of execution from the last day of the month of January, that is, 31 January, and then 28 February. See the **Nominal Time** column in the web console. If you remember, nominal time is the exact scheduled time for the job to run. Actual time is the time at which the job ran in reality. Since we started backdated job, all the old instances are running slowly now:

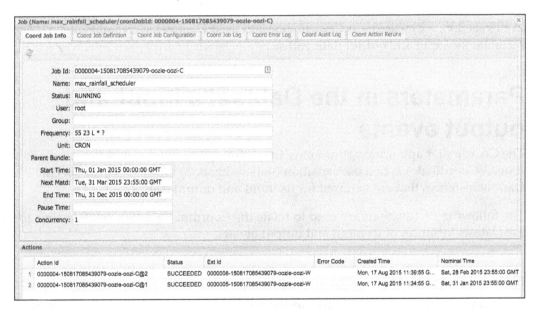

Oozie web console Coordinator v1

We can verify the output for the execution by browsing the path `hadoop fs -cat /user/hue/learn_oozie/ch05/processed/max_rainfall/`.

This is same as output path defined in our Coordinator and `dataset.xml`.

The Coordinator dynamically calculates the inputs and output paths for each instance of execution of the Workflow. Each month, one path is calculated and passed onto the Workflow for execution, as shown in the following screenshot:

```
[root@sandbox ch05]# hadoop fs -ls /user/hue/learn_oozie/ch05/processed/max_rainfall/
Found 1 items
drwxr-xr-x   - root hdfs          0 2015-08-17 12:05 /user/hue/learn_oozie/ch05/processed/max_rainfall/2015
[root@sandbox ch05]# hadoop fs -ls /user/hue/learn_oozie/ch05/processed/max_rainfall/2015/
Found 7 items
drwxr-xr-x   - root hdfs          0 2015-08-17 11:35 /user/hue/learn_oozie/ch05/processed/max_rainfall/2015/01
drwxr-xr-x   - root hdfs          0 2015-08-17 11:40 /user/hue/learn_oozie/ch05/processed/max_rainfall/2015/02
drwxr-xr-x   - root hdfs          0 2015-08-17 11:45 /user/hue/learn_oozie/ch05/processed/max_rainfall/2015/03
drwxr-xr-x   - root hdfs          0 2015-08-17 11:50 /user/hue/learn_oozie/ch05/processed/max_rainfall/2015/04
drwxr-xr-x   - root hdfs          0 2015-08-17 11:55 /user/hue/learn_oozie/ch05/processed/max_rainfall/2015/05
drwxr-xr-x   - root hdfs          0 2015-08-17 12:00 /user/hue/learn_oozie/ch05/processed/max_rainfall/2015/06
drwxr-xr-x   - root hdfs          0 2015-08-17 12:05 /user/hue/learn_oozie/ch05/processed/max_rainfall/2015/07
[root@sandbox ch05]# hadoop fs -ls /user/hue/learn_oozie/ch05/processed/max_rainfall/2015/01
Found 2 items
-rw-r--r--   1 root hdfs          0 2015-08-17 11:35 /user/hue/learn_oozie/ch05/processed/max_rainfall/2015/01/_SUCCESS
-rw-r--r--   1 root hdfs         12 2015-08-17 11:35 /user/hue/learn_oozie/ch05/processed/max_rainfall/2015/01/part-r-00000
[root@sandbox ch05]# hadoop fs -cat /user/hue/learn_oozie/ch05/processed/max_rainfall/2015/01/part-r-00000
2015,1,11.0
[root@sandbox ch05]# 
```

Rainfall output Coordinator v1

In this section, we created our Coordinator and used Datasets to dynamically calculate the input and output data paths.

Parameters in the Dataset's input and output events

The Coordinator application runs many times during the span of start time and end time. A Coordinator action uses creation (materialization) time to find the specific Dataset instances that are required for its input and output events.

The following EL functions are used to relate the Coordinator action creation time to the Dataset instances of its input and output events.

current(int n)

The current(int n) function gives us the *n*th Dataset instance for a synchronous Dataset, relative to the Coordinator action creation time.

For example, current(1) represents the instance, which is calculated after adding the start time with the frequency.

In our case, `current(1)` of rainfall is resolved to `/user/hue/learn_oozie/ch05/input/rainfall/2015/01`. This was resolved at the end of month of January.

```
<data-in name="wf_input" dataset="rainfall">
  <instance>${coord:current(0)}</instance>
</data-in>
```

We can also use negative *n*, for example:

```
<data-in name="inputraindata" dataset="rainlogs">
  <start-instance>${coord:current(-23)}</start-instance>
  <end-instance>${coord:current(0)}</end-instance>
</data-in>
```

In the preceding example, it would be all the instances of last 24 hours (assume `rainlogs` has a frequency of hours).

hoursInDay(int n)

The `hoursInDay(int n)` function returns the number of hours for the specified day, taking into consideration timezone/daylight savings.

daysInMonth(int n)

The `daysInMonth(int n)` function returns the number of days for the month of the specified day.

latest(int n)

The `latest(int n)` function represents the *n*th latest currently available instance of a synchronous Dataset.

Read more about EL functions for datasets at `https://oozie.apache.org/docs/4.2.0/CoordinatorFunctionalSpec.html#a6.6._Parameterization_of_Dataset_Instances_in_Input_and_Output_Events`.

Change the Coordinator used here to have the calculation done for last two months in one go, instead of one month at a time.

If you noticed, when we started the Coordinator that was backdated, Oozie spawned multiple executions. Many times, you do not want that to happen. For example, if the job is fetching full snapshot of the database from Oracle via Sqoop and you have a delay in Oozie jobs, you might not want to refresh the full snapshot multiple times when you know that you are not getting additional benefit with running additional jobs. This reminds me of one project story.

At regular intervals, we had to plan out the downtime of the Hadoop cluster. There were many reasons, for example, firmware upgrade, Hadoop distribution upgrade, disk replacement, and so on. On all these occasions, we used our script to pause and restart the jobs. Often when an Oozie Coordinator job runs, it calculates the possible runnable instances of the Workflow. When we restarted jobs after cluster downtime, all of those instances that were eligible to run used to bombard the cluster with jobs. For example, if the cluster was down for one day, the hourly job would have a queue of each hour eligible. Waiting for jobs to clear up the production platform queue for humans to use was a much awaited activity after each downtime. This is the story of the older Oozie version when we did not have option to decide the Coordinator action execution policy, which we are going to discuss next.

Coordinator controls

The execution policies for the actions of a Coordinator job can be defined in the Coordinator application. There are different types of Coordinator controls, as shown in the following figure:

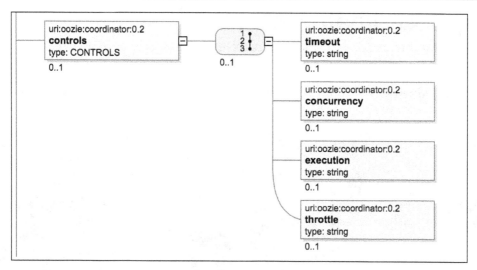

Coordinator controls

Here's a brief explanation of the Coordinator controls present in the preceding figure:

- **timeout**: The timeout control allows us to say how long the Coordinator action will be in the `waiting` or `ready` state before timing out on its execution, for example, five minutes.

- **concurrency**: Using this control, we can specify the concurrency for the Coordinator actions. It specifies how many Coordinator actions are allowed to run concurrently (the `running` status).

- **execution**: If there is a backlog of Coordinators, this control helps to decide which one should be executed. The different choices are oldest first (`FIFO`), newest first (`LIFO`), none (`NONE`), and last one only (`LAST_ONLY`).

- **throttle**: The throttle control specifies the maximum number of Coordinator actions that are allowed to be in the `waiting` state at the same time.

We will revise our Coordinator with the controls that we discussed to have timeout, concurrency, execution strategy, and throttle value.

Pig Coordinator job v3

The code for this section is available at BOOK_CODE_HOME/learn_oozie/ch05/
rainfall/v3.

We have defined all the controls, as shown in lines 4-9 in the following screenshot.
The corresponding property file is passing the updated values:

```xml
1  <coordinator-app name="max_rainfall_scheduler_v3" frequency="${frequency}"
2                   start="${start_date}" end="${end_date}" timezone="Australia/Sydney"
3                   xmlns="uri:oozie:coordinator:0.4">
4    <controls>
5      <timeout>${timeout}</timeout>
6      <concurrency>${concurrency_level}</concurrency>
7      <execution>${execution_order}</execution>
8      <throttle>${materialization_throttle}</throttle>
9    </controls>
10
11   <datasets>
12       <include>${data_definitions}</include>
13   </datasets>
14   <input-events>
15     <data-in name="wf_input" dataset="rainfall">
16       <instance>${coord:current(0)}</instance>
17     </data-in>
18   </input-events>
19   <output-events>
20     <data-out name="wf_output" dataset="max_rainfall">
21       <instance>${coord:current(0)}</instance>
22     </data-out>
23   </output-events>
24
25   <action>
26     <workflow>
27       <app-path>${wf_application_path}</app-path>
28       <configuration>
29         <property>
30           <name>input</name>
31           <value>${coord:dataIn('wf_input')}</value>
32         </property>
33         <property>
34           <name>output</name>
35           <value>${coord:dataOut('wf_output')}</value>
36         </property>
37       </configuration>
38     </workflow>
39   </action>
40 </coordinator-app>
```

... gitbook ▸ oozie ▸ learn_oozie ▸ ch05 ▸ rainfall ▸ v3 ▸ coordinator.xml   UTF-8   XML   Ln: 1

Pig Coordinator v3

The updated `job.properties` file is as follows:

```
# Time and schedule details
start_date=2015-01-01T00:00Z
end_date=2015-12-31T00:00Z
frequency=55 23 L * ?
nameNode=hdfs://sandbox.hortonworks.com:8020
# Workflow to run
wf_application_path=hdfs://sandbox.hortonworks.com:8020/user/hue/
learn_oozie/ch05/rainfall/v3
# Coordinator to run
oozie.coord.application.path=hdfs://sandbox.hortonworks.com:8020/
user/hue/learn_oozie/ch05/rainfall/v3
# Datasets
data_definitions=hdfs://sandbox.hortonworks.com:8020/user/hue/
learn_oozie/ch05/rainfall/datasets/datasets.xml
# Controls
timeout=10
concurrency_level=1
execution_order=LAST_ONLY
materialization_throttle=1
```

Trigger the job using the following command:

```
oozie job -run job.properties
```

Not that the execution order has been set to LAST_ONLY. Let's check the web console to note how our jobs are running:

Oozie web console skipped

Since we were running the job in back date, Oozie skipped all the instances as we have instructed it to run only the last needed jobs.

Summary

We covered lot of ground in this chapter. We started with creation of Pig action Workflow and simple Pig command-line execution. Then, we started creating a Coordinator for our Pig job and discussed the concepts of EL functions in data input and output instances along with control options.

In the next chapter, we will discuss the concept of parameterization of Coordinator application by using another case study and examples. We will also see how to run Hive jobs from Oozie.

6
Running Hive Jobs

In this chapter, we will see how to run Hive jobs from Oozie. As part of concept building, we will talk about parameterization of Coordinator application actions.

In this chapter, we will:

- Run Hive action from Oozie
- Run Hive 2 action jobs from Oozie

From the concept point of view, we will:

- Understand the concept parameterization of Coordinator application actions

Chapter case study

We will continue to build on the previous chapter's case study, in which we calculated the maximum rainfall in each month. We will insert the output of Pig script in Hive table, which will allow people to query it as and when needed.

We will start off by running Oozie Hive job via the command-line option and later see the Hive action in Workflow.

Running a Hive job from the command line

We can submit the Oozie Hive job from the command line. To see the Oozie help menu, we need to pass the arguments shown in the following screenshot:

```
      oozie hive <OPTIONS> -X <ARGS> : submit a hive job, everything after '-X' are pass-t
hrough parameters to hive, any '-D' arguments after '-X' are put in <configuration>
              -auth <arg>            select authentication type [SIMPLE|KERBEROS]
              -config <arg>          job configuration file '.properties'
              -D <property=value>    set/override value for given property
              -doas <arg>            doAs user, impersonates as the specified user
              -file <arg>            hive script
              -oozie <arg>           Oozie URL
              -P <property=value>    set parameters for script
```

Hive command-line options

The code for this section of chapter is present in the `hive_commandline` file placed at `<BOOK_CODE_HOME>/learn_oozie/ch06/`.

The Hive script used is pretty simple. It is just loading data into the Hive table using the LOAD command as follows:

```
LOAD DATA INPATH '/user/hue/learn_oozie/ch06/hive_commandline/input'
INTO TABLE CH06_RAINFALL_TREND;
```

To run the job, we can use the following command:

```
oozie hive -config job.properties -file Insert.hql -oozie
http://localhost:11000/oozie
```

Check the status of the job in the Oozie web console. The job should finish successfully.

In the next section, we will see the Hive action of Oozie.

Hive action

The general schema for Hive action is as follows:

```
<action>
    <job-tracker>        // Job tracker details
    <name-node>          // Name node details
    <prepare>            // Create or Delete directory
    <job-xml>            // Any job xml properties
    <configuration>      // Hadoop job configuration
    <script>             // Hive script to run
    <param>              // Parameters to hive script
    <argument>           // Arguments
    <file>               // Any files needed to run job
    <archive>            // Any job dependencies (jar etc)
</action>
```

Check out the location `BOOK_CODE_FOLDER/xsd_svg/hive-action-0.5.svg` to see the visual representation.

 In the Oozie versions above v4.2, Hive action also supports running the Hive query instead of file-based script arguments.

We will start off from where we left in the previous chapter. We will persist the maximum rainfall, which we calculated in each month in the Hive table. So, our data flow would be to process files by Pig action and save results to the Hive table.

Let's create the Workflow.

As per our use case, we have two actions: `max_rainfall`, which is a Pig action, and a Hive action named `hive`. The code for this section of book is present in the folder `<BOOK_CODE_HOME>/learn_oozie/ch06/v1/workflow.xml`. The following screenshot shows the code present in `workflow.xml`:

```
1  <workflow-app name="max_rainfall_ch06_v1" xmlns="uri:oozie:workflow:0.5">
2
3  <global>
4     <job-tracker>${jobTracker}</job-tracker>
5     <name-node>${nameNode}</name-node>
6  </global>
7
8  <start to="max_rainfall"/>
9
10 <action name="max_rainfall">
11    <pig>
12       <prepare>
13          <delete path="${output}"/>
14       </prepare>
15       <script>/user/hue/learn_oozie/ch05/rainfall/pig/max_rain.pig</script>
16       <param>pig_input=${input}</param>
17       <param>pig_output=${output}</param>
18    </pig>
19    <ok to="hive"/>
20    <error to="Kill"/>
21 </action>
22
23 <action name="hive">
24    <hive xmlns="uri:oozie:hive-action:0.5">
25       <script>${hivescript}</script>
26          <param>inputHive=${inputHive}</param>
27          <param>outputHiveTable=${outputHiveTable}</param>
28    </hive>
29    <ok to="End"/>
30    <error to="Kill"/>
31 </action>
32
33 <kill name="Kill">
34    <message>Action failed, error message[${wf:errorMessage(wf:lastErrorNode())}]</message>
35 </kill>
36
37 <end name="End"/>
38 </workflow-app>
```

hive_workflow_v1

See the use of the `<global>` tag in lines 3 to 6. We are passing the Hive script name, input Hive data path, and output Hive table name as parameters from the property file.

We are using the following Hive script:

```
LOAD DATA INPATH '${hivevar:inputHive}' INTO TABLE
${hivevar:outputHiveTable};
```

The property file for the previous Workflow is shown as follows:

```
# Workflow to run
oozie.wf.application.path=hdfs://sandbox.hortonworks.com:8020/user/
hue/learn_oozie/ch06/v1
# Parameters for Pig
input=/user/hue/learn_oozie/ch05/input/
output=/user/hue/learn_oozie/ch05/output/rainfall_pig_workflow
# Hive action
hivescript=/user/hue/learn_oozie/ch06/v1/hive/insert.hql
inputHive=/user/hue/learn_oozie/ch05/output/rainfall_pig_workflow
outputHiveTable=CH06_RAINFALL_TREND
```

Copy the preceding code to HDFS if not done at the start of book.

Let us run the Oozie Workflow using the following command:

```
cd <BOOK_CODE_HOME/learn_oozie/ch06/v1>
oozie job -config job.properties -config http://localhost:11000/oozie
```

On the web console, check the status of the job once it gets submitted. After completing the job successfully, log in to Hive and check that the data has been inserted to your Hive table. Open the SSH terminal to your virtual machine and open the Hive shell using the following commands:

```
# Start Hive
hive
# Show the data
hive>select * from CH06_RAINFALL_TREND;
```

You can see the output in the following screenshot:

```
hive> select * from CH06_RAINFALL_TREND;
OK
2015    1       12.0
2015    2       13.0
2015    3       11.0
2015    4       22.0
2015    5       24.0
2015    6       9.0
2015    7       8.0
2015    8       7.0
```

hive_workflow_output_v1

Exercise: Create a new Workflow in which you select all the records from the CH06_RAINFALL_TREND table and store it in the HDFS directory of your choice.

The role of other elements like prepare, archive, file, and configuration is same as we discussed previously. We can delete or create directories in prepare steps, provide any external jars needed to run the Oozie action (for example, UDFs) in the archive element, and so on.

This completes our first interaction with Hive action execution using Oozie. We executed the Hive action to insert data in the Hive table.

Validating Oozie Workflow

Oozie also provides the command to validate the Workflow before submitting. If there is some schema error in the XML, Oozie will say that Workflow is not valid. Just execute the oozie validate command in the directory where you have your workflow.xml or coordinator.xml files. In the example shown in the following screenshot, there was XML syntax issue. Due to change in order of the job-tracker declaration in the global element Oozie, we get a message saying that there is issue in validation:

```
[root@sandbox v1]# oozie job -run -config job.properties
Error: E0701 : E0701: XML schema error, cvc-complex-type.2.4.a: Invalid content
was found starting with element 'job-tracker'. One of '{"uri:oozie:workflow:0.5"
:job-xml, "uri:oozie:workflow:0.5":configuration}' is expected.
[root@sandbox v1]# oozie validate workflow.xml
Error: Invalid app definition, org.xml.sax.SAXParseException; lineNumber: 4; col
umnNumber: 18; cvc-complex-type.2.4.a: Invalid content was found starting with e
lement 'job-tracker'. One of '{"uri:oozie:workflow:0.5":job-xml, "uri:oozie:work
flow:0.5":configuration}' is expected.
[root@sandbox v1]# oozie validate workflow.xml
Valid workflow-app
[root@sandbox v1]#
```

oozie_validate_workflow

 Exercise: Log in to HUE and create the same Workflow using Hue Workflow editor.

Hive 2 action

Oozie also has Hive 2 action, where we can use Hive Server 2 and execute our Hive queries. Hive 2 action uses Beeline to execute queries via the Hive Server 2.

Here's the general command to talk to the Beeline server:

```
beeline> !connect jdbc:hive2://localhost:10000 username password
org.apache.hive.jdbc.HiveDriver
```

 To know more about how Beeline and Hive Server 2 work, check out the Cloudera website blog post at http://blog.cloudera.com/blog/2014/02/migrating-from-hive-cli-to-beeline-a-primer/.

The general schema for Hive action is as follows:

```
<action>
  <job-tracker>        // Job tracker details
  <name-node>          // Name node details
  <prepare>            // Create or Delete directory
  <job-xml>            // Any job xml properties
  <configuration>      // Hadoop job configuration
  <jdbc-url>           // HiveServer2 JDBC URL
  <password>           // Password (if any for Hiveserver2)
  <script>             // Hive script to run
  <param>              // Parameters to hive script
  <argument>           // Arguments
  <file>               // Any files needed to run job
  <archive>            // Any job dependencies (jar etc)
</action>
```

 If you are using Hive versions older than 0.13, then using more than one --hivevar flag does not work. For more information, visit https://issues.apache.org/jira/browse/HIVE-6045.

The code for this section of the chapter is present in the folder <BOOK_CODE_HOME>/learn_oozie/ch06/v2.

The revised Workflow to use Hive 2 action is as follows:

```
<workflow-app name="max_rainfall_ch06_v2"
xmlns="uri:oozie:workflow:0.5">
  <global>
    <job-tracker>${jobTracker}</job-tracker>
    <name-node>${nameNode}</name-node>
  </global>
  <start to="max_rainfall"/>
    <action name="max_rainfall">
      <pig>
        <prepare>
          <delete path="${output}"/>
        </prepare>
        <script>/user/hue/learn_oozie/ch05/rainfall/
        pig/max_rain.pig</script>
        <param>pig_input=${input}</param>
        <param>pig_output=${output}</param>
      </pig>
      <ok to="hive2"/>
      <error to="Kill"/>
    </action>
    <action name="hive2">
      <hive2 xmlns="uri:oozie:hive2-action:0.1">
        <jdbc-url>${hivejdbcurl}/${outputHiveDatabase}</jdbc-url>
        <script>${hivescript}</script>
        <param>outputHive=${outputHive}</param>
      </hive2>
      <ok to="End"/>
      <error to="Kill"/>
    </action>
    <kill name="Kill">
    <message>Action failed, error
    message[${wf:errorMessage(wf:lastErrorNode())}]</message>
  </kill>
  <end name="End"/>
</workflow-app>
```

 I have skipped the password as my test virtual machine is configured not to have a password for running Hive queries. However, if your cluster has a password authentication (for example, LDAP), then you can enter the password as well.

The property file provides the location of Hive script as follows:

```
# Job.properties file
# Workflow to run
oozie.wf.application.path=hdfs://sandbox.hortonworks.com:8020/user
/hue/learn_oozie/ch06/v2
# Parameters for Pig
input=/user/hue/learn_oozie/ch05/input/
output=/user/hue/learn_oozie/ch05/output/rainfall_pig_workflow
# Hive2 action
hivescript=/user/hue/learn_oozie/ch06/v2/hive/insert.hql
outputHive=/user/hue/learn_oozie/ch06/v2/output/
rainfall_hive2action_workflow
outputHiveDatabase=default
```

Submit and run the job by using the following command:

```
oozie job -config job.properties -oozie http://localhost:11000/oozie
```

Check the status of the Oozie job in the web console and after it completes, check for data in the output location.

We will shift gear now and learn about parameterization of Coordinator jobs.

Parameterization of Coordinator jobs

These functions are used to control Datasets, which are used for processing or produced as part of Coordinator processing.

dateOffset(String baseDate, int instance, String timeUnit)

This function calculates the datestamp based on the following calculation:

newDateStamp = baseDateStamp + (instance*timeUnit)

It offsets the *baseDateStamp* value by the amount given by instance and *timeUnit*.

The *timeUnit* value can be one of the following:

- YEAR
- MONTH
- DAY
- HOUR
- MINUTE

Consider the following example:

```
${coord:dateOffset(coord:nominalTime(), 2, 'DAY')}
```

If nominal time is `2015-08-22T23:00Z`, then after the new calculation the output will be `2015-08-24T23:00Z`.

dateTzOffet(String baseDate, String timezone)

This function calculates the datestamp based on the following calculation:

newDateStamp = baseDateStamp + (Oozie Processing Timezone - Given Timezone)

It offsets the *baseDateStamp* value by the difference from Oozie processing timezone to the timezone passed as argument.

You can see the list of supported timezones that can be passed as argument using the following command:

```
oozie info -timezones
```

Consider the following example:

```
${coord:dateTzOffset(coord:nominalTime(), "Australia/Sydney")}
```

formatTime(String timeStamp, String format)

This function converts the `timeStamp` string in one format to another format. One of the use cases is to convert the ISO8601 timeStamp into other desired formats.

The argument of format should be written as per convention of SimpleDateFormat. You can check out the standard timestamp formats from the Java API at `https://docs.oracle.com/javase/8/docs/api/java/text/SimpleDateFormat.html`.

For example, if `timeStamp` is `2015-08-22T00:00Z` and argument of the format is `yyyy`, the output will be `2015`.

The `formatTime()` function is used extensively in calculating the `where` clause of Sqoop imports or Hive queries.

Consider the following example:

```
Select * from table where account_date=${coord:formatTime(String
timeStamp, String yyyyMMdd)}
```

Summary

In this chapter, we saw how to run Hive queries from Oozie along with the new Hive 2 action, which allows us to run Hive Server 2 JDBC queries. After that, we also covered Coordinator parameterization functions for datasets.

In the next chapter, we will see how to import data into Hadoop using Sqoop and schedule those jobs via Oozie.

Summary

7
Running Sqoop Jobs

In this chapter, we will see how to run the Sqoop jobs from Oozie. Sqoop (SQL to Hadoop) is used to import and export data from different database systems on to the Hadoop platform.

In this chapter, we will:

- Run Sqoop jobs from the command line
- Create Oozie Workflow for Sqoop actions
- Run Sqoop jobs from Coordinators

From the concept point of view, we will:

- Understand the concept of HCatalog Datasets
- Understand HCatalog Coordinator and EL functions

Chapter case study

Let's have a twist in the rainfall use case we solved in the previous chapter. Instead of getting CSV files for rainfall data, we need to import the rainfall data from MySQL database and then move on to processing.

As the first step of the analysis, we need to bring data inside Hadoop using Sqoop. To do this, we will use Sqoop import at end of each day to get data on Hadoop, and then we will run our Pig script for processing and saving results to Hive.

Just like previous chapters, we will start with the command-line option to trigger jobs, and we will learn about Sqoop action and scheduling it via Coordinator. Lastly, we will cover the concept of HCatalog Datasets. Let's get started.

Running Sqoop command line

The syntax for the Oozie Sqoop command-line execution is shown in the following screenshot:

```
oozie sqoop <OPTIONS> -X <ARGS> : submit a sqoop job, everything after '-X' are pass-through parameters to sqoop,
any '-D' arguments after '-X' are put in <configuration>
              -auth <arg>             select authentication type [SIMPLE|KERBEROS]
              -command <command>      sqoop command
              -config <arg>           job configuration file '.properties'
              -D <property=value>     set/override value for given property
              -doas <arg>             doAs user, impersonates as the specified user
              -oozie <arg>            Oozie URL
```

Sqoop command line

Let's import all records for the table to HDFS.

 For sample MySQL database preparation, I have created one script in the folder <BOOK_CODE_HOME>/ch07/sqoop_commandline/ loadToMySQL.sh, using which you can create one database to test the Sqoop import.

The database name is rainfall and table is rainfall_data. We can import all the records from this table using the Sqoop command-line import option. To create the test Dataset, execute the steps written in loadToMySQL.sh.

We are ready to run the job. I have saved the following command in the script <BOOK_CODE_HOME>/ch07/sqoop_commandline/import_all_records.sh:

```
oozie sqoop -oozie http://localhost:11000/oozie -command import --
connect jdbc:mysql://localhost:3306/rainfall --username root --
password "" --table rainfall_data --target-dir
'/user/hue/learn_oozie/ch07/sqoop_commandline/rainfall/output' -m
1 -config job.properties
```

Sqoop needs the JDBC driver libraries to do the import. So any third-party JAR files that are needed (for example, Teradata, Netezza, Greenplum, and so on) should be copied in the oozie.libpath variable declared in the property file. As a best practice, we should have single libpath for all Workflows.

The corresponding job.properties file is shown here:

```
jobTracker=sandbox.hortonworks.com:8050
mapreduce.jobtracker.address=sandbox.hortonworks.com:8050
fs.defaultFS=hdfs://sandbox.hortonworks.com:8020
nameNode=hdfs://sandbox.hortonworks.com:8020
oozie.use.system.libpath=True
```

```
oozie.libpath=hdfs://sandbox.hortonworks.com:8020/user/hue/
learn_oozie/ch07/sqoop_commandline/lib
```

Note the `libpath` variable declared here and also note that I have already copied the MySQL JDBC JAR in the path `/user/hue/learn_oozie/ch07/sqoop_commandline/lib`. Depending on the database from where you are going to import you should add the required JAR in `libpath`.

Let's run the preceding job using the following command and wait for it to complete:

cd <BOOK_CODE_HOME>/ch07/sqoop_commandline/import_all_records.sh

Note the job ID generated by Oozie and see the corresponding Workflow generated by Oozie using the following command:

oozie job -definition 0000034-150905021502101-oozie-oozi-W

Replace the preceding ID with the ID that was shown to you.

The job starts immediately on submission and once it is finished, we can see the data inside HDFS. Check out the following screenshot:

```
[root@sandbox sqoop_commandline]# ./run.sh
job: 0000028-150905021502101-oozie-oozi-W
[root@sandbox sqoop_commandline]# hadoop fs -ls /user/hue/learn_oozie/ch07/sqoop_commandline/rainfall/output
Found 2 items
-rw-r--r--   1 root hdfs          0 2015-09-05 07:38 /user/hue/learn_oozie/ch07/sqoop_commandline/rainfall/output/_SUCCESS
-rw-r--r--   1 root hdfs       8001 2015-09-05 07:38 /user/hue/learn_oozie/ch07/sqoop_commandline/rainfall/output/part-m-00000
[root@sandbox sqoop_commandline]# hadoop fs -cat /user/hue/learn_oozie/ch07/sqoop_commandline/rainfall/output/part-m-00000
IDCJAC0009,086282,2015,1,1,0.0,0,0.0
IDCJAC0009,086282,2015,1,2,0.0,0,0.0
IDCJAC0009,086282,2015,1,3,0.0,0,0.0
IDCJAC0009,086282,2015,1,4,3.2,1,0.0
IDCJAC0009,086282,2015,1,5,0.0,0,0.0
IDCJAC0009,086282,2015,1,6,0.0,0,0.0
IDCJAC0009,086282,2015,1,7,0.0,0,0.0
IDCJAC0009,086282,2015,1,8,1.8,1,0.0
```

Sqoop job to import all records

Using the Sqoop command-line option, we can import data from databases when we have to do it as a one-time job. To schedule such kind of jobs regularly using Coordinator, we have to use Sqoop action, which we will see in the next section.

Exercise: Import selected records using Sqoop `freeform` import from the command-line option using the `where` clause. Check out the example in `<BOOK_CODE_HOME>/ch07/sqoop_commandline/sqoop_freeform.sh`.

Sqoop action

Sqoop action allows us to include the Sqoop commands as part of the broader Workflow, which can be part of data pipeline. All the parameters that Sqoop needs can be configured via XML arguments.

Open the Sqoop SVG diagram at `<BOOK_CODE_HOME>/xsd_svg/sqoop-action-0.4` and see the different properties and elements required for Sqoop action to work.

Check out the following SVG:

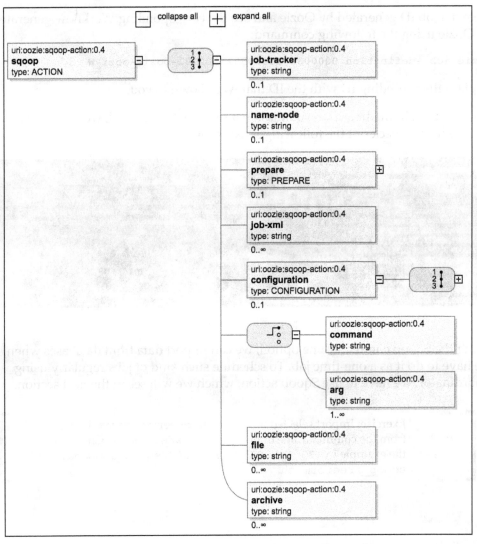

Sqoop action SVG

Most of the elements required for Sqoop action are similar to the ones we have already seen. The main definition of Sqoop action can be done with one of the two options:

- command
- arg

An example of the command option is as follows:

```
<command>import --connect jdbc:mysql://localhost/database --
username sqoop --password sqoop --table tablenameinDB --hive-
import --hive-table tablnameinHive</command>
```

Here's an example of an arg option:

```
<arg>import</arg>
<arg>--connect</arg>
<arg>jdbc:mysql://localhost</arg>
<arg>--username</arg
<arg>root</arg>
<arg>--password</arg>
<arg>""</arg>
<arg>--query</arg>
<arg>"select * from tableName"</arg>
<arg>--target-dir</arg>
<arg>hdfsFolder</arg>
<arg>-m</arg>
<arg>4</arg>
<arg>--direct</arg>
```

You can change the preceding arguments, for example, tableName, password, hdfsFolder, and mappers, as per your requirements.

To see a practical example, we will modify our previous chapter Workflow, add the Sqoop action as starting point, and then call the Pig action. Further, we will also push this data to Hive. To send data to Hive table, we will not use Hive action. We will use the HCatalog-based Datasets approach to make it interesting.

The general data flow of our problem will be as follows:

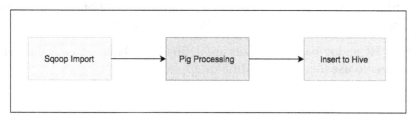

Sqoop, Pig processing, and Hive insertion Workflow

Before we start the actual example, let's discuss some concepts related to HCatalog and HCatalog-backed datasets. This is a new feature added to Oozie 4.x release.

HCatalog

HCatalog provides the table and storage management layer for Hadoop. It brings various tools in the Hadoop ecosystem together. Using HCatalog interface, different tools like Hive, Pig, and MapReduce can read and write data on Hadoop. All of them can use the shared schema and datatypes provided by HCatalog. Having shared the mechanism of reading and writing makes it easy to consume the output of one tool in the other one.

So how does HCatalog come in section of Datasets? So far, we have seen the HDFS folder-based Datasets in which based on some success flag, we come to know that data is available. Using HCatalog-based Datasets, we can trigger Oozie jobs based on time when data in a given Hive partition becomes available for consumption. This takes Oozie to the next level of job dependency, where we can consume data as and when it is available in Hive.

To quickly see an example of interoperability, let's see how Pig can use Hive tables and how HCatalog brings all tools together. Read the comments (lines with #) as you read the code:

```
# Start Pig and add Hcatalog jars to Pig classpath
$ pig -useHCatalog
# Load Our Hive table in Pig
grunt> A = LOAD 'ch06_rainfall_trend'
using org.apache.hive.hcatalog.pig.HCatLoader();
# Describe Table
grunt> describe A;
A: {year: int,month: int,rainfall: float}
# Now data of Hive table can be accessed and used by relation A
inside Pig
grunt>
```

You can find more information on HCatalog on Wikipedia at https://cwiki.apache.org/confluence/display/Hive/HCatalog+UsingHCat.

Let's see how HCatalog-based Datasets are defined and later we will see various options on how to use them in Coordinator applications.

HCatalog datasets

HCatalog uses Hive metastore to provide table-layer abstraction to different tools such as Pig, MapReduce, and so on, and it allows access to data stored in Hive. The Datasets can be defined as HCatalog by using the following general syntax:

```
hcat://HiveMetastoreURL/hiveDatabaseName/hiveTableName/
HiveTablePArtitionInformation
```

To see one concrete example, see the following Dataset declaration for table named `rainfall_partitioned`:

```
<datasets>
  <dataset name="rainfall_partitioned"
  frequency="${coord:months(1)}" initial-instance="2015-01-
01T00:00Z" timezone="Australia/Sydney">
    <uri-template>hcat://${hcaturl}/default/ch07_v1_max_rainfall_
    trend/yearmonth=${YEAR}${MONTH}</uri-template>
    <done-flag></done-flag>
  </dataset>
</datasets>
```

The code for this section of book is present at `<BOOK_CODE_HOME>/learn_oozie/ch07/datasets`.

It is similar to file-based Datasets with a change in `<uri-template>`. The DDL for the table `ch07_v1_max_rainfall_trend` is shown here to make it clear. Note the relation between database name, tablename, partition information in Dataset, and DDL.

After Pig has done the processing, we will store our results in a Hive table named `ch07_v1_max_rainfall_trend`. This table can be directly accessed from Pig using the following commands:

```
-- Code <BOOK_CODE_HOME>/learn_oozie/ch07/v1/hive/Create_table.hql
CREATE TABLE default.ch07_v1_max_rainfall_trend (RAINFALL FLOAT)
PARTITIONED BY (YEARMONTH INT)
ROW FORMAT DELIMITED
FIELDS TERMINATED BY ','
LOCATION '/user/hue/learn_oozie/ch07/v1/max_rainfall_trend/output';
```

The partition pattern matches with what we have declared in Dataset. There is only one column in the table, but that does not influence our learning of Oozie.

HCatalog EL functions

There is one HCatalog EL function that can be used to check if a given HCatalog partition (Hive partition) exists or not:

```
boolean hcat:exists(String uri)
```

Here's an example:

```
hcat:exists("hcat://${hcaturl}/default/ch07_v1_max_rainfall_trend/
yearmonth=${YEAR}${MONTH}")
```

This example, at runtime, might resolve to:

```
hcat:exists("hcat://localhost:10000/default/ch07_v1_max_rainfall_
trend/yearmonth=201501")
```

HCatalog Coordinator functions

There are many HCatalog Coordinator functions. A brief summary of each of them is given in the following table:

Function	Use
databaseIn(String name)	Returns input database name for the HCatalog Dataset
databaseOut(String name)	Returns output database name for the HCatalog Dataset
tableIn(String name)	Returns input table name for the HCatalog Dataset
tableOut(String name)	Returns output database name for the HCatalog Dataset
dataInPartitionFilter(String name, String type)	Filters the Hive partitions and returns the required Dataset to be consumed by Pig, Hive, or Java actions
dataOutPartitions(String name)	Comma-separated list of output partitions
dataInPartitionMin(String name, String partition)	Minimum value for partition in given input event instances
dataInPartitionMax(String name, String partition)	Maximum value for partition in given input event instances
dataOutPartitionValue(String name, String partition)	Returns the value of partition for output event
dataInPartitions(String name, String type)	List of key-value pairs for the input event Dataset

We will see the example of a few of them as we move along in this chapter.

Exercise: Take a short break from reading this book and look at the official documentation. Read about all the HCatalog functions at `http://oozie.apache.org/docs/4.2.0/ CoordinatorFunctionalSpec.html#a6.8_Using_HCatalog_ data_instances_in_Coordinator_Applications_since_ Oozie_4.x`. Each of them is very well explained with example.

Let's get back to the case study for our chapter. We decided that the flow of data will be from Sqoop import to Pig processing to Hive table.

To insert the data from Pig to Hive, we will use the newly learned concept of HCatalog and Pig integration.

A section of the Workflow is shown in the following screenshot:

```
10    <action name="sqoop_import">
11      <sqoop xmlns="uri:oozie:sqoop-action:0.4">
12        <prepare>
13          <delete path="${pig_base_input}/${year}/${month}"/>
14        </prepare>
15        <arg>import</arg>
16        <arg>--connect</arg>
17        <arg>jdbc:mysql://${mysqlurl}</arg>
18        <arg>--username</arg>
19        <arg>root</arg>
20        <arg>--password</arg>
21        <arg>""</arg>
22        <arg>--query</arg>
23        <arg>${query}</arg>
24        <arg>--target-dir</arg>
25        <arg>${pig_base_input}/${year}/${month}</arg>
26        <arg>-m</arg>
27        <arg>1</arg>
28        <arg>--direct</arg>
29      </sqoop>
30      <ok to="max_rainfall"/>
31      <error to="Kill"/>
32    </action>
33
34    <action name="max_rainfall">
35      <pig>
36        <script>${pig_script}</script>
37        <param>pig_input=${pig_base_input}/${year}/${month}</param>
38        <param>pig_output_db=${pig_output_db}</param>
39        <param>pig_output_table=${pig_output_table}</param>
40        <param>yearmonth=${yearmonth}</param>
41        <file>${hive_site}</file>
42      </pig>
43      <ok to="End"/>
44      <error to="Kill"/>
45    </action>
```

Sqoop Workflow

The code for this section of chapter is present at `<BOOK_CODE_HOME>/learn_oozie/ch07/v1/workflow.xml`.

In the Sqoop action, we use the `arg` method. In line 15 of the preceding Workflow, we declare that it is a Sqoop import job and then we declare various arguments needed by Sqoop import, one in each line. If you try to pass multiple arguments in a single line, the Workflow will throw an error. Try to do that and see the results.

> **Exercise**: Convert the preceding Sqoop action to a command type of Sqoop action.

Pig script

The Pig script, which is calculating the maximum rainfall each month, is shown in the following screenshot:

```
1  A = load '${pig_input}' using PigStorage(',') as
      (product_code:chararray,station_number:long,year:int,month:int,day:int,rainfall:float,period_in_days:int,quality:
      chararray);
2  B = GROUP A BY (year,month);
3  C = foreach B generate MAX(A.rainfall) as rainfall;
4  STORE C INTO '${pig_output_db}.${pig_output_table}' using
      org.apache.hive.hcatalog.pig.HCatStorer('yearmonth=${yearmonth}');
```

Pig processing

Note the input variables needed by the Pig script. It needs `pig_input` (line 1). It also needs database, tablename, and partition (line 4) information for storing output.

The job.properties file

As best practice, we have moved all the parameters in external property file. Check out the property file given here. One of the important properties is `oozie.libpath`. Sqoop needs external JDBC JAR to work. To add it to the classpath of the job, we can either drop in the `lib` folder inside or keep it in `oozie.libpath`. We have used both of these approaches in the examples given in the following screenshot:

```
1  # Parameters for workflow
2
3  query="select * from rainfall.rainfall_data where year='${year}' AND month='${month}' AND $CONDITIONS"
4  pig_base_input=/user/hue/learn_oozie/ch07/input/rainfall
5  pig_script=/user/hue/learn_oozie/ch07/v1/pig/max_rain.pig
6  hive_site=/user/hue/learn_oozie/ch07/v1/hive-site.xml
7  oozie.libpath=hdfs://sandbox.hortonworks.com:8020/user/hue/learn_oozie/ch07/sqoop_commandline/lib
8
9  # Time and schedule details
10 start_date=2015-01-01T00:00Z
11 end_date=2015-12-31T00:00Z
12 frequency=55 23 L * ?
13
14 nameNode=hdfs://sandbox.hortonworks.com:8020
15 hcaturl=localhost:10000
16
17 # Workflow to run
18 wf_application_path=hdfs://sandbox.hortonworks.com:8020/user/hue/learn_oozie/ch07/v1
19 # Coordinator to run
20 oozie.coord.application.path=hdfs://sandbox.hortonworks.com:8020/user/hue/learn_oozie/ch07/v1
21
22 # Datasets
23 data_definitions=hdfs://sandbox.hortonworks.com:8020/user/hue/learn_oozie/ch07/datasets/datasets.xml
24
25 # Controls
26 timeout=10
27 concurrency_level=1
28 execution_order=FIFO
29 materialization_throttle=1
```

The job.properties file

Check out the JAR files present at `<BOOK_CODE_HOME>/learn_oozie/ch07/v1/lib`.

The query for Sqoop is defined in line 3. Note the presence of two variables, `${year}` and `${month}`; both of them will be passed on by Coordinator depending on the year and month for which the job is being run.

The path where Sqoop will import data has been defined in line 4. This path will be combined with the year and month to calculate the fully qualified unique path of each month. Again, the Coordinator will pass on this dynamic information to Workflow.

For example, see line 25 of the Sqoop Workflow:

`${pig_base_input}/${year}/${month}`

This will resolve to `/user/hue/learn_oozie/ch07/input/rainfall/2015/01` for the month of January and so on.

Another important property to note is `hcaturl`, which is same as the Hive metastore URL. This has been defined in line 15 in the properties file, shown in the preceding screenshot.

The Sqoop action Coordinator

Let's see the Coordinator that will run our Workflow regularly to import data from database using Sqoop. The code for this section is available at <BOOK_CODE_HOME>/ learn_oozie/ch07/v1/coordinator.xml.

I would like to repeat our problem statement and what we are trying to do. Every day, the rainfall records are stored in the MySQL. At the end of each month, we import those records to HDFS using Sqoop. Then, we run Pig code to find highest rainfall in that month and store the results in a Hive table.

You can see that we defined the Coordinator frequency as monthly (this is not shown in the screenshot; please see the code folder). We defined the output Hive table as a HCatalog Dataset and that Dataset is being declared in the Coordinator which is at line 12 of the following screenshot:

```xml
11  <datasets>
12      <include>${data_definitions}</include>
13  </datasets>
14
15  <output-events>
16    <data-out name="wf_output" dataset="rainfall_partitioned">
17        <instance>${coord:current(0)}</instance>
18    </data-out>
19  </output-events>
20
21  <action>
22    <workflow>
23      <app-path>${wf_application_path}</app-path>
24      <configuration>
25        <property>
26          <name>year</name>
27          <value>${coord:formatTime(coord:nominalTime(),"yyyy")}</value>
28        </property>
29        <property>
30          <name>month</name>
31          <value>${coord:formatTime(coord:nominalTime(),"MM")}</value>
32        </property>
33        <property>
34          <name>pig_output_db</name>
35          <value>${coord:databaseOut('wf_output')}</value>
36        </property>
37        <property>
38          <name>pig_output_table</name>
39          <value>${coord:tableOut('wf_output')}</value>
40        </property>
41        <property>
42          <name>yearmonth</name>
43          <value>${coord:dataOutPartitionValue('wf_output','yearmonth')}</value>
44        </property>
45      </configuration>
46    </workflow>
47  </action>
48 </coordinator-app>
```

Coordinator

As an example, please see how the different EL functions resolve on first run at the end of the month of January 2015. Note the line numbers in column 1, code in column 2, and what output that code will generate in column 3:

Line no	Code	Output
17	`current(0)`	`hcat://localhost:10000/default/ch07_v1_max_rainfall_trend/yearmonth=201501"`
27	`formatTime(coord:nominalTime(),"yyyy")`	2015
31	`formatTime(coord:nominalTime(),"MM")`	01
35	`databaseOut('wf_output')`	`default`
39	`tableOut('wf_output')`	`ch07_v1_max_rainfall_trend`
43	`dataOutPartitionValue('wf_output','yearmonth')`	`yearmonth='201501'`

The Coordinator passes all of them as arguments to the Workflow. Take some time and relate it to Workflow. You should start at `config-default.xml`, then `job.properties`, and then move to `coordinator.xml`, `dataset.xml`, and `workflow.xml`.

Running the job

I am assuming that you have already copied all the source code of the book to HDFS at the start of this book. If not, please do so now.

Let's run the job using the following commands:

```
$ cd <BOOK_CODE_HOME>/learn_oozie/ch07/v1/
$ oozie job -run -config job.properties
```

After some time, Oozie will start executing the first instance of the job for the month of January 2015. Note that all of them are backlog jobs and in our Coordinator properties, we have defined the execution policy as FIFO. As a result, all backlog jobs will be run by the Coordinator one by one.

To check the progress of the job, we can go to the web console to verify the job status, as shown in the following screenshot:

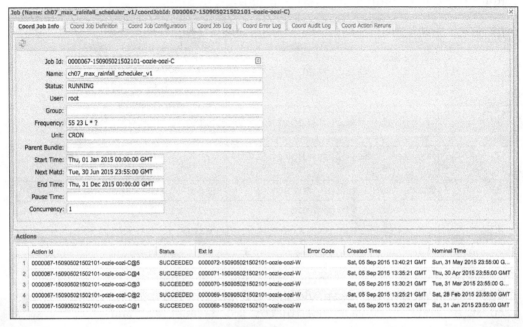

Oozie web console success

Checking data in the Hive table

To verify that data is being inserted properly in Hive tables, we can use the Hive select count query as shown in the following screenshot:

```
Time taken: 0.282 seconds, Fetched: 5 row(s)
hive> select * from ch07_v1_max_rainfall_trend;
OK
11.0    201501
21.4    201502
16.8    201503
10.2    201504
5.6     201505
Time taken: 0.269 seconds, Fetched: 5 row(s)
hive>
```

Hive table import check

Summary

This completes our chapter. We discussed the new concept of HCatalog and Oozie integration, which has been recently released. We also covered Sqoop action and used the concepts that we discussed in the previous chapters to make a Coordinator.

In the next chapter, we will see how to run Spark jobs from Oozie.

8
Running Spark Jobs

In this chapter, we will see how to run Spark jobs from Oozie. Spark has changed the whole ecosystem of Hadoop and the Big Data world. It can be used as ETL tool or machine learning tool, and it can be used where traditionally we use Pig, Hive, or Sqoop.

In this chapter, we will:

- Create Oozie Workflow for Spark actions

From the concept point of view, we will:

- Understand the concept of Bundles

We will start off with a simple Workflow in which we will rewrite the same Pig logic of finding maximum rainfall in a given month in Spark and then we will schedule that using Oozie Workflow and Coordinators. The idea is to show the beauty of Spark—how seamlessly it replaces various tools such as Pig or Hive, and how it has become the default execution engine of the Big Data platform. If you are a very keen follower of Hadoop news, recently Cloudera announced that they are declaring phase out of MapReduce and are going to keep all their eggs in the Spark bucket. The vast number of open-pull requests (`https://github.com/apache/spark/pulls`) shows how everyone is excited about this tool. We cannot discuss the details about Spark, its architecture, and why it is gaining so much popularity in this book. However, I would recommend you to go to the Spark website (`https://spark.apache.org`) and read about it.

Spark action

The Spark action has been recently added in Oozie and the general XSD is shown in the following figure:

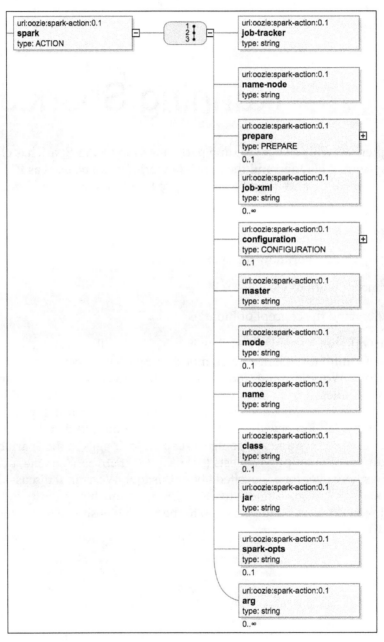

Spark SVG action

The general schema is as follows:

```
<action>
    <job-tracker>          // Job tracker details
    <name-node>            // Name node details
    <prepare>              // Create or Delete directory
    <job-xml>              // Any job xml properties
    <configuration>        // Hadoop job configuration
    <master>               // Spark master details
    <mode>                 // Spark driver mode
    <name>                 // Spark Job name
    <class>                // Spark main class
    <spark-opts>           // Spark Job options
    <arg>                  // Arguments for the job
</action>
```

The `<master>` element tells about the URL of Spark master. Spark can run in different cluster configurations, namely Spark standalone, Mesos, and Yarn. Depending on which cluster manager you are using, the master URL will change. For example, `spark://host:port` for Spark standalone, `mesos://host:port` when the cluster manager is Mesos, `yarn-cluster://host:port` or `yarn-master://host:port` when the cluster manager is Yarn, or `local://host:port` when you are testing jobs on a local machine.

The `<mode>` element tells about the mode of spark driver execution. The Spark driver can run inside the cluster (mode as cluster) and on the client machine where the job has been submitted (mode as client).

The `<spark-opts>` element is optional. If present, it can have a list of spark options that will be passed to the Spark driver. The configuration can be specified in the format `--conf key=value` in this element or it can also be configured in `oozie-site.xml` under `oozie.service.SparkConfigurationService.spark.configurations`. However, the `spark-opts` configs have priority over the `oozie-site.xml` settings.

In Hortonworks virtual machine, we have Spark running on top of Yarn. Based on that, we will use the settings for the Yarn-managed Spark cluster.

I have already written some Spark code to simulate what was done by the Pig script to convert the raw data of rainfall to a processed form. The code for this section is available at `<BOOK_CODE_HOME>/learn_oozie/ch08`.

The Spark code is in the `rainbow` folder, which we will package as JAR and use in our Oozie Workflow. Start the Spark service in Ambari console if it's not running. You can also follow along if you are running the Cloudera or other Hadoop distribution. I have used Spark 1.3.1 in the following code example, but this does not change how we use Oozie to schedule our Spark jobs:

```
cd /learn_oozie/ch08/rainbow
mvn clean compile package assembly:single
```

Wait for Maven to download all the dependencies and build uber JAR for us.

Once the process is complete, we can see JAR under the folder <BOOK_CODE_HOME>/ learn_oozie/ch08/rainbow/target/rainbow-1.0.0-jar-with-dependencies. jar.

We will test it quickly via the command line to see how it works (I assume you have already copied the code to HDFS at the start of this book):

```
spark-submit \

--master "yarn-cluster" \

--class "life.jugnu.learnoozie.ch08.MaxRainfall" \

<BOOK_CODE_HOME>/learn_oozie/ch08/rainbow/target/rainbow-1.0.0-
jar-with-dependencies.jar \

/user/hue/learn_oozie/ch05/input/rainfall/2015/01/Rainfall-2015-
01.txt /tmp/ch08/rainbow
```

There are two arguments for the Scala class `life.jugnu.learnoozie.ch08.` `MaxRainfall`; one is input path `/user/hue/learn_oozie/ch05/input/` `rainfall/2015/01/Rainfall-2015-01.txt` and other is output path `/tmp/ch08/` `rainbow`.

Wait for the job to finish and then see the output in HDFS by running the following command:

```
hadoop fs -cat /tmp/ch08/rainbow/part-00000
```

The output should be as follows:

```
2015,1,11.0
```

Let's create the Oozie Workflow for running this regularly.

The Spark action for the command line we executed earlier is shown here:

```
<spark xmlns="uri:oozie:spark-action:0.1">
  <job-tracker>${jobTracker}</job-tracker>
  <name-node>${nameNode}</name-node>
  <master>yarn-cluster</master>
  <mode>cluster</mode>
  <name>Spark Ch08 Max Rain Calculator</name>
  <class>life.jugnu.learnoozie.ch08.MaxRainfall</class>
  <jar>/user/hue/learn_oozie/ch08/rainbow/target/rainbow-1.0.0-
jar-with-dependencies.jar</jar>
  <arg>${input}</arg>
  <arg>${output}</arg>
</spark>
```

The code for this section is available in the folder `<BOOK_CODE_HOME>/learn_oozie/ch08/spark_rainfall`.

Submit the Workflow for execution using the Oozie job submit command as follows:

`oozie job -run -config job.properties`

The job will start running as soon as it is submitted. Wait for the job to complete and check the final output under `/user/hue/learn_oozie/ch08/processed/max_rainfall`.

There are a few important things to keep in mind here:

- Oozie needs to be built with the same version of Spark which you are using in your code
- If your job fails with a `class not found` exception, then check the version of Spark used in your code and what libraries are present in the Oozie shared library
- By default, Oozie comes with Spark 1.1
- Check out the Hadoop distribution documentation to know more about the versions and compatibility

You can also override the action shared library if there is a version conflict. For more information, check out the Oozie documentation at `https://oozie.apache.org/docs/4.2.0/WorkflowFunctionalSpec.html#a17.1_Action_Share_Library_Override_since_Oozie_3.3`.

[**Exercise**: Schedule Spark Workflow to use the Python script.]

Bundles

So far, you've learned about Workflows (what to do) and Coordinators (when to do) in Oozie.

Now we will cover Bundles. Bundles are a group of Coordinators that are grouped together and managed all as one bundle. This makes it easy to operate set of Coordinators to start, stop, and resume the jobs.

The basic SVG diagram for the Bundles is shown here:

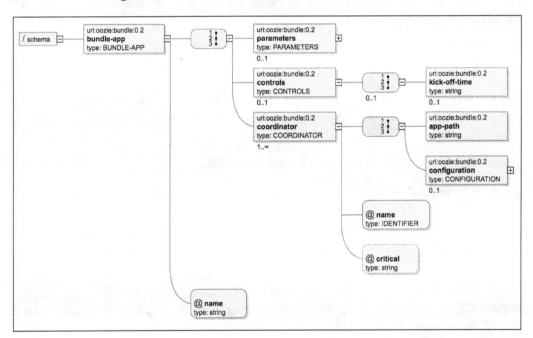

Bundles specification

Bundle needs to have information about the set of Coordinators for which it is responsible and the kick-off time. Kick-off time is the time at which Bundle should start and submit all the applications to the Oozie server. The Coordinators which are a part of a Bundle may or may not have a relationship between them. They can be part of the same or different data pipelines. Generally, the best practice is to bundle all tables that are coming from the same database, or bundle all Coordinators that are part of same data pipeline.

You might want to check out the pictorial representation of Bundle's job flow on this blog:

```
http://hadooped.blogspot.com.au/2013/07/apache-oozie-part-10-bundle-
jobs.html
```

The general schema of Bundle is as follows:

```
<bundle-app>            // Start of Bundle app
  <parameters>         // Parameters
  <controls>           // Controls as Kick-off-time
  <kick-off-time>
  <coordinator>        // Coordinators definitions ( one or more)
  <app-path>
  <configuration>
</bundle-app>
```

For example, we will just use the Coordinators made in the previous chapter and run them together as part of a Bundle.

Note the kick-off time at which we defined that this Bundle should start and submit both of the Coordinators for execution. The code is as follows:

```
<bundle-app name="Sample Bundle Example"
xmlns:xsi="http://www.w3.org/2001/XMLSchema-instance"
xmlns="uri:oozie:bundle:0.2">
  <parameters>
    <property>
      <name>oozie.use.system.libpath</name>
      <value>true</value>
    </property>
  </parameters>
  <controls>
   <kick-off-time>2015-03-11T15:22Z</kick-off-time>
  </controls>
  <coordinator name="Coordinator_Ch05_rainfall_v3">
    <app-path>${nameNode}/user/hue/learn_oozie/ch05/rainfall/v3
    </app-path>
    <configuration>
      <property>
        <name>wf_application_path</name>
        <value>${nameNode}/user/hue/learn_oozie/ch05/rainfall/v3</
        value>
      </property>
      <property>
        <name>data_definitions</name>
        <value>${nameNode}/user/hue/learn_oozie/ch05/rainfall/
        datasets/datasets.xml</value>
```

```
          </property>
        <property>
          <name>frequency</name>
          <value>55 23 L * ?</value>
        </property>
        <property>
          <name>execution_order</name>
          <value>LAST_ONLY</value>
        </property>
        <property>
          <name>start_date</name>
          <value>${start_date_1}</value>
        </property>
        <property>
          <name>end_date</name>
          <value>${end_date_1}</value>
        </property>
      </configuration>
    </coordinator>
    <coordinator name="Coordinator_Ch05_rainfall_v2">
      <app-path>${nameNode}/user/hue/learn_oozie/ch05/rainfall/v2</app-
      path>
      <configuration>
        <property>
          <name>wf_application_path</name>
          <value>${nameNode}/user/hue/learn_oozie/ch05/rainfall/v2</
          value>
        </property>
        <property>
          <name>frequency</name>
          <value>55 23 L * ?</value>
        </property>
        <property>
          <name>start_date</name>
          <value>${start_date_2}</value>
        </property>
        <property>
          <name>end_date</name>
          <value>${end_date_2}</value>
        </property>
      </configuration>
    </coordinator>
  </bundle-app>
```

Like Workflow and Coordinator, Bundle too has a job.properties file that defines the properties. The only new property in the following property file is oozie.bundle.application.path, which defines the location of bundle.xml in the HDFS:

```
# Time and schedule details
frequency=55 23 L * ?
nameNode=hdfs://sandbox.hortonworks.com:8020

# Datasets
data_definitions=hdfs://sandbox.hortonworks.com:8020/user/hue/
learn_oozie/ch05/rainfall/datasets/datasets.xml

# Controls
timeout=10
concurrency_level=1
materialization_throttle=1

# This defines location on HDFS where bundle is stored
oozie.bundle.application.path=hdfs://sandbox.hortonworks.com:8020/
user/hue/learn_oozie/ch08/bundles/
start_date_1=2015-01-01T00:00Z
end_date_1=2015-12-31T00:00Z
start_date_2=2015-01-01T00:00Z
end_date_2=2015-12-31T00:00Z
```

Let's submit and run this job using the following commands:

```
cd <BOOK_CODE_HOME>/learn_oozie/ch08/bundles
oozie job -run -config job.properties
```

The job will start immediately and we can see its progress in the Oozie web console:

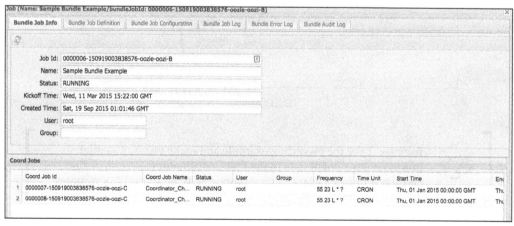

Bundle Oozie web console

Click on any Coordinator to see the execution of the Workflow.

Data pipelines

In real Big Data projects, the Coordinators are scheduled tasks that are part of the data pipeline. For example, get data from some system and process it (this forms one Coordinator), and then another sub process can send the processed data to a database (this forms another Coordinator). Finally, both of them are abstracted to form Bundle. To think in terms of how to solve your job using Oozie, start by drawing the job Workflow on a whiteboard/paper. Then discuss with your team how you can create unit abstractions to run individually and in isolation.

Check out the following example.

The database has a record of daily rainfall in Melbourne. We import that data to Hadoop using a regular Coordinator job (Coordinator 1). Using another scheduled job, we send the results back to the database as shown in the following figure:

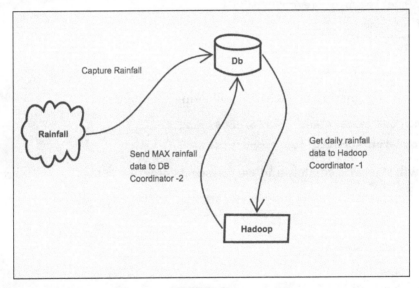

Data pipelines

 Exercise: Take the preceding example and make one Bundle that processes our rainfall data in the first Coordinator (using Pig script) and sends the data as part of Sqoop export in the second Coordinator.

Summary

In this chapter, we saw how to run Apache Spark jobs from Oozie. Then, we discussed how to think in terms of data pipelines and finally discussed Bundles.

In the next chapter, we will talk about various production-related concepts and day-to-day tasks that are helpful while running Oozie.

Running Oozie in Production

9

In this chapter, we will see how to deploy Oozie code in production using best practices of continuous integration and deployment. We will also see how to make Oozie work in a secured Hadoop cluster. Besides this, we will discuss how to restart the Oozie jobs that have failed in between.

In this chapter, we will:

- Create production-ready code for Oozie

From the concept point of view, we will:

- Understand the concept of rerun

Packaging and continuous delivery

In this section, we will see how to package the Oozie code and deploy it in production.

The code for this section is available in the folder `<BOOK_CODE_HOME>/learn_oozie/ch09/packaging`.

Import the project in to your favorite editor (Eclipse/Intellij) as a Maven project.

The source code of Oozie gets deployed at two places:

- On HDFS, where we copy all the Workflows, Coordinators, and so on.
- On the local client machine from where we submit the jobs using the command line. All the `job.properties` files reside here.

If you see the code folder, we have a simple Maven project in which we have the following folder structure:

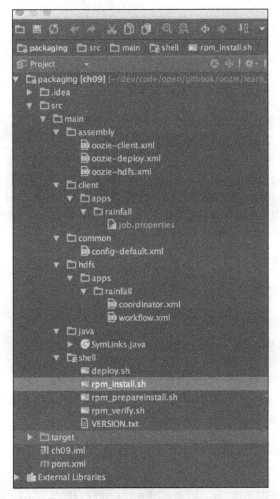

Maven project structure

We can see that the code that goes to HDFS has been written in the hdfs folder, and the code that has to be on the local client machine has been written in the client folder. Under both of them, we have a folder called apps. Under apps, we have different apps representing Oozie Workflows. I have copied one of the applications named rainfall, which we made previously. You can have more apps under this folder as you add various production Oozie implementations. I have shared an example here.

The `config-default` file is a common file that is needed by each app.

There is a folder named `assembly` that has Maven assemblies that package the code for client and HDFS deployments.

For example, check out the following `oozie-hdfs.xml` assembly:

```
<assembly>
  <id>hdfs</id>
  <formats>
    <format>dir</format>
    <format>zip</format>
  </formats>
  <includeBaseDirectory>false</includeBaseDirectory>
  <fileSets>
    <fileSet>
      <directory>${basedir}/src/main/hdfs</directory>
      <outputDirectory>hdfs/hdfs-${project.version}</outputDirectory>
    </fileSet>
  </fileSets>
  <files>
    <file>
      <source>src/main/common/config-default.xml</source>
      <outputDirectory>hdfs/hdfs-${project.version}/apps/rainfall
      </outputDirectory>
    </file>
    <file>
      <source>target/classes/VERSION.txt</source>
      <outputDirectory>hdfs/hdfs-${project.version}</outputDirectory>
    </file>
  </files>
</assembly>
```

The preceding assembly packages the code in the `hdfs` folder in to the output folder called `hdfs`. The `config-default.xml` file is copied to the app `rainfall`. The `VERSION.txt` file is also copied, which gives us a handy way to find the current version of code installed in production.

If you have Maven installed on your machine, then you can build the project by using the following command:

```
mvn clean package assembly:single
```

After the build is complete, go to the folder named `target`. The following packages are built:

- `ch09-1.0.0-client.zip`
- `ch09-1.0.0-deploy.zip`
- `ch09-1.0.0-hdfs.zip`

The `client` package can be extracted to the client machine. The `hdfs` package can be copied to `hdfs`.

To do both of the preceding deployments, we have to deploy the `zip` package. Extract and see the contents of `deploy.zip`. It is a simple shell script.

To do real production implementation conforming to continuous integration and deployment principles, we have the following Workflow:

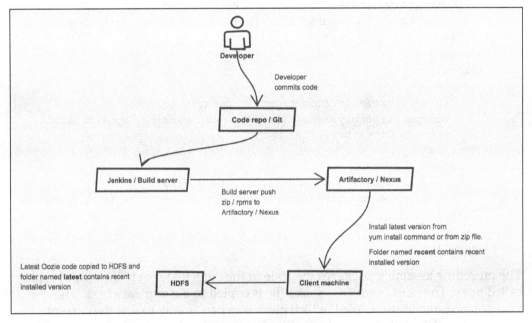

Continuous deployment

The following is an explanation of the preceding figure:

1. First, the developer commits the code to the git repo (or svn).
2. The build server (Jenkins) builds the code and packages it into the ZIP/RPM files.
3. The ZIP/RPM files are copied to Artifactory/Nexus.

4. On the client machine, we use the `deploy` script to manually install the code on client and HDFS.

5. Use the simple `yum install oozie-essentials` command to automatically install the latest version of the code, picking the required RPMs from Artifactory/Nexus.

To build the RPM artifacts that can be deployed, the build server needs to have the `rpm-build` package installed. On Redhat/CentOS, we can install this using following command:

```
yum install rpm-build
```

The code can be packaged using the following Maven command:

```
mvn package assembly:single rpm:attached-rpm
```

You can see the generated RPM at `BOOK_CODE_HOME/learn_oozie/ch09/` `packaging/target/rpm/oozie-essentials/RPMS/noarch/`.

To install RPM, we can use the `yum localinstall rpm_name` command. If the repository is added as yum repo to the client machine, we can also use the yum install oozie-essentials command. The following screenshot shows confirmation of installation:

```
[root@sandbox noarch]# pwd
/media/sf_jagatsingh/GitBook/Library/jagatsingh/oozie/learn_oozie/ch09/packaging/target/rpm/oozie-essentials/RPMS/noarch
[root@sandbox noarch]# yum localinstall oozie-essentials-1.0.0-1.noarch.rpm
Failed to set locale, defaulting to C
Loaded plugins: fastestmirror, priorities
Setting up Local Package Process
Examining oozie-essentials-1.0.0-1.noarch.rpm: oozie-essentials-1.0.0-1.noarch
Marking oozie-essentials-1.0.0-1.noarch.rpm to be installed
Loading mirror speeds from cached hostfile
 * base: centos.mirror.digitalpacific.com.au
 * epel: ucmirror.canterbury.ac.nz
 * extras: mirror.nsw.coloau.com.au
 * updates: centos.mirror.digitalpacific.com.au
Resolving Dependencies
--> Running transaction check
---> Package oozie-essentials.noarch 0:1.0.0-1 will be installed
--> Finished Dependency Resolution

Dependencies Resolved

========================================================================================================================
 Package               Arch           Version           Repository                              Size
========================================================================================================================
Installing:
 oozie-essentials      noarch         1.0.0-1           /oozie-essentials-1.0.0-1.noarch        13 k

Transaction Summary
========================================================================================================================
Install       1 Package(s)

Total size: 13 k
Installed size: 13 k
Is this ok [y/N]: █
```

RPM installation

After the installation is complete, check the status of the files copied to HDFS. I have configured the code deployment location to /tmp/dev/applications, but you can configure any path. Following screenshot shows the status of the files copied:

```
[root@sandbox tmp]# hadoop fs -ls -R /tmp/dev/applications
drwxr-xr-x   - oozie hdfs          0 2015-09-26 06:55 /tmp/dev/applications/oozie
drwxr-xr-x   - oozie hdfs          0 2015-09-26 06:55 /tmp/dev/applications/oozie/code
drwxr-xr-x   - oozie hdfs          0 2015-09-26 06:55 /tmp/dev/applications/oozie/code/latest
-rw-r--r--   1 oozie hdfs         13 2015-09-26 06:55 /tmp/dev/applications/oozie/code/latest/VERSION.txt
drwxr-xr-x   - oozie hdfs          0 2015-09-26 06:55 /tmp/dev/applications/oozie/code/latest/apps
drwxr-xr-x   - oozie hdfs          0 2015-09-26 06:55 /tmp/dev/applications/oozie/code/latest/apps/rainfall
-rw-r--r--   1 oozie hdfs        775 2015-09-26 06:55 /tmp/dev/applications/oozie/code/latest/apps/rainfall/config-default.xml
-rw-r--r--   1 oozie hdfs       1142 2015-09-26 06:55 /tmp/dev/applications/oozie/code/latest/apps/rainfall/coordinator.xml
-rw-r--r--   1 oozie hdfs        759 2015-09-26 06:55 /tmp/dev/applications/oozie/code/latest/apps/rainfall/workflow.xml
[root@sandbox tmp]# hadoop fs -cat /tmp/dev/applications/oozie/code/latest/VERSION.txt
version=1.0.0[root@sandbox tmp]#
```

HDFS installation status check

To check the currently running version of code, we can always cat the VERSION.txt file using the following command:

```
hadoop fs -cat /tmp/dev/applications/oozie/code/latest/VERSION.txt.
```

This gives the latest version installed in HDFS. Check the last line in the preceding screenshot to confirm the version:

```
[root@sandbox oozie]# pwd
/tmp/dev/install/oozie
[root@sandbox oozie]# tree
.
`-- client
    |-- client-1.0.0
    |   |-- VERSION.txt
    |   `-- apps
    |       `-- rainfall
    |           `-- job.properties
    `-- latest -> /tmp/dev/install/oozie/client/client-1.0.0

5 directories, 2 files
[root@sandbox oozie]#
```

Client installation check

Similarly, we can check the version of the client installed using the following command:

```
cat /tmp/dev/install/oozie/client/latest/VERSION.txt
```

To submit this job, let's go to the folder where client has the job.properties files installed using the following command:

```
cd /tmp/$OOZIE_CODE_ENV/install/oozie/client/latest/apps/rainfall
oozie job -run -config job.properties  -Denv=$OOZIE_CODE_ENV
```

Note how we are passing the environment variable using $OOZIE_CODE_ENV to the execution. You can also set this in the environment variable, for example, bash_profile for a user who is executing the Oozie command.

You do not need $OOZIE_CODE_ENV if you have physically separate test, development, and production environments. But many times we only have logical environments and one physical environment. In such situations, this helps to test the code before moving to production.

Oozie in secured cluster

A Hadoop cluster, which has been secured, needs some additional configuration for Oozie to work properly. The standard actions like Pig or MapReduce do not need any additional configuration from the Oozie side to run. However, when Oozie needs to talk to external services such as HBase, HCatalog, and Hive2 Server, we need to know how to authenticate them.

This is done by providing information about credentials for the security. Oozie has provided implementation for authentication for different external tools like Hive, HBase, and HCat.

In oozie-site.xml, we need to add the following code:

```
<property>
  <name>oozie.credentials.credentialclasses</name>
  <value>
    hcat=org.apache.oozie.action.hadoop.HCatCredentials,
    hbase=org.apache.oozie.action.hadoop.HbaseCredentials,
    hive2=org.apache.oozie.action.hadoop.Hive2Credentials
  </value>
</property>
```

In workflow.xml, we need to state that we want to use the declared credentials and pass additional details about where the external service is. The following table shows the details of various services:

Service	Details
hcat	hcat.metastore.principal and hcat.metastore.uri
hbase	hbase-site.xml
hive2	hive2.server.principal and hive2.jdbc.url

For example, the revised Workflow for `<BOOK_CODE_HOME>/learn_oozie/ch06/v3/ workflow.xml` for running in a secured cluster will be as follows:

```
1  <workflow-app name="max_rainfall_ch06_v3" xmlns="uri:oozie:workflow:0.5">
2
3      <credentials>
4          <credential name='hcat-creds' type='hcat'>
5              <property>
6                  <name>hcat.metastore.uri</name>
7                  <value>HCAT_URI</value>
8              </property>
9              <property>
10                  <name>hcat.metastore.principal</name>
11                  <value>HCAT_PRINCIPAL</value>
12              </property>
13          </credential>
14      </credentials>
15
16      <start to="max_rainfall"/>
17
18      <action name="max_rainfall" cred='hcat-creds'>
19          <pig>
20              <job-tracker>${jobTracker}</job-tracker>
21              <name-node>${nameNode}</name-node>
22              <script>${pig_script}</script>
23              <param>pig_input=${pig_input}</param>
24              <param>pig_output_db=${pig_output_db}</param>
25              <param>pig_output_table=${pig_output_table}</param>
26              <param>yearmonth=${yearmonth}</param>
27              <file>${hive_site}</file>
28          </pig>
29          <ok to="End"/>
30          <error to="Kill"/>
31      </action>
32
```

HCat crendentials Kerberos

In the lines 3 to 14 in the preceding screenshot, we declared the `hcat-creds` (you can use any name) and stated that it is of type `hcat`. This maps to the type we defined in `oozie-site.xml` earlier. To use it, we passed it to our Pig action (line 18), since the Pig script is using the HCat access to push data to Hive.

In case of Hive, we will need to pass on `hive2.server.principal` and `hive2.jdbc url`.

To learn about the Kerberos principle, visit `http://web.mit.edu/kerberos/krb5-1.5/krb5-1.5.4/doc/krb5-user/What-is-a-Kerberos-Principal_003f.html`.

Ask your Hadoop cluster administrator about the principle details for HCat, HBase, and Hive2. Generally, it is of the form `Service/fully.qualified.domain.name@ YOUR-REALM.COM`.

An example with Oozie interacting with HBase cluster is given as follows.

In Workflow credentials, we declare the following code:

```
<credentials>
  <credential name='hbaseauth' type='hbase'>
  </credential>
</credentials>
```

In the action, which is talking to HBase, we just pass the credentials:

```
<action name="process" cred="hbaseauth">
```

We also need to add details about `hbase-site.xml`:

```
<job-xml>${hbaseSite}</job-xml>
<file>${hbaseSite}#hbase-site.xml</file>
```

A complete example is shown here:

```
<action name="hbaseprocess" cred="hbaseauth">
  <java>
    <job-tracker>${jobTracker}</job-tracker>
    <name-node>${nameNode}</name-node>
    <job-xml>${hbaseSite}</job-xml>
    <configuration>
      <property>
        <name>mapred.job.queue.name</name>
        <value>${queueName}</value>
      </property>
    </configuration>
    <main-class>${process_classname}</main-class>
    <file>${hbaseSite}#hbase-site.xml</file>
    <capture-output/>
  </java>
  <ok to="success"/>
  <error to="failed"/>
</action>
```

This completes the section on running Oozie in a secured Hadoop environment. Before moving on to next section of reruns, it is time for a story.

Our machine learning scoring job was very long running (I don't know what the data scientist had coded, that's why they earn a lot). Due to having a large customer base of 30 million and a large number of features, the scoring on average used to take 6 hours to finish. One fine Thursday, we had planned a production change for the scoring algorithm. The change was done in the early morning so that we could monitor progress throughout the day. When the scoring was about to finish, the Oozie job failed after 5 hours of work. We checked all the logs to find why the processing had failed. After our analysis, we found the root cause was a mismatch in JAR in our development and production environments (sounds like you heard of this problem?). This was for processing which happens after scoring action. We did not want to rerun the full Oozie job starting from the initial phase and sit in office for another 6 hours (making it a long day of 14 hours). We used Oozie's ability to trigger jobs from failed actions: the Oozie rerun. The general syntax is `oozie job -rerun <jobid> -Doozie. wf.rerun.failnodes=true`. We will cover the Oozie rerun in the next section.

Rerun

Life is not perfect! Every day we have to face failures and same is with Oozie running in production. Jobs fail and we need to rerun them.

Oozie provides a functionality to restart the jobs from intermediate states to save time:

- To rerun a Coordinator, we need to tell about the action which has failed or the date for which we need to rerun

- To rerun a Bundle, we need to tell about Coordinator which has failed

Rerun Workflow

To rerun a Workflow that has failed, we have two nodes:

- `oozie.wf.rerun.skip.nodes`

- `oozie.wf.rerun.failnodes`

`oozie.wf.rerun.skip.nodes` is the list of nodes to skip, while `oozie.wf.rerun.failnodes` is a Boolean value that tells if Oozie should run only the failed nodes.

Here's an example of Workflow rerun:

```
oozie job -rerun 0000003-150921003038748-oozie-oozi-W -
Doozie.wf.rerun.failnodes=true
```

In the preceding example, we passed on the ID of Workflow to rerun.

Rerun Coordinator

To rerun a Coordinator that has failed, we need to tell about the actions to rerun or tell about the date (in UTC) for which we need to rerun the Coordinator.

The general command is as follows:

```
oozie job -rerun <coord_Job_id> [-nocleanup] [-refresh] [-failed]
[-config <arg>]
```

Here's a sample execution:

```
oozie job -rerun 0000002-150920023900085-oozie-oozi-C -action 1-3
```

The following screenshot shows the output of the preceding command:

```
[root@sandbox rainfall]# oozie job -rerun 0000002-150920023900085-oozie-oozi-C
Error: Invalid options provided for rerun: date or action expected.
[root@sandbox rainfall]# oozie job -rerun 0000002-150920023900085-oozie-oozi-C -action 1-3
Action ID          Nominal Time
-----------------------------------------------------------------------------------------
0000002-150920023900085-oozie-oozi-C@1   2015-01-31 23:55 UTC
0000002-150920023900085-oozie-oozi-C@2   2015-02-28 23:55 UTC
0000002-150920023900085-oozie-oozi-C@3   2015-03-31 23:55 UTC
[root@sandbox rainfall]#
```

Coordinator rerun

Rerun Bundle

To rerun the Bundle job that failed, we need to tell about Coordinator to rerun date (in UTC).

The general command is as follows:

```
oozie job -rerun <bundle_Job_id> [-coordinator <list of coordinator
name separate by comma>
```

Here's a sample execution:

```
oozie job -rerun 0000006-150919003838576-oozie-oozi-B -coordinator
0000007-150919003838576-oozie-oozi-C
```

For more information, visit the following links:

Workflow rerun-https://oozie.apache.org/docs/4.2.0/
DG_WorkflowReRun.html

Coordinator rerun-https://oozie.apache.org/docs/4.2.0/
CoordinatorFunctionalSpec.html#a14._Coordinator_
Rerun

Bundle rerun-https://oozie.apache.org/docs/4.2.0/
BundleFunctionalSpec.html#a8._Bundle_Rerun

Summary

In this chapter, we saw how to package and deploy the Oozie code in production. Then we discussed how to configure Oozie code to run in a secured cluster. You also learned about the concept of rerun. I am sure you will be a pro with Oozie.

Index

D

DAG
  URL 23
data pipelines
  defining 128
Datasets
  <done-flag> tag 65
  cron syntax, for frequency 62, 63
  defining 58-60
  frequency and time 61
  timezone 64
daylight savings
  URL 64
Decision node
  defining 41
Directed Acyclic Graphs (DAGs)
  about 1
  URL, for wikipedia 1

E

EL functions, for datasets
  URL 85
Email action
  configuration, defining 45
  defining 41
  URL 42
Expression Language functions
  basic EL constants 42, 43
  defining 42
  Hadoop EL constants 43
  HDFS EL functions 44
  types 42
  workflow EL functions 43

H

Hadoop
  use cases 24
HCatalog
  defining 108
  HCatalog Coordinator functions 110-112
  HCatalog datasets 109
  HCatalog EL functions 110
  job.properties file 112, 113
  Pig script 112
  Sqoop action Coordinator 114, 115

HCatalog Coordinator functions
  defining 110-112
HCatalog datasets 109
HCatalog EL functions 110
Hive 2 action
  defining 97-99
Hive action 93-96
Hive job
  running, from command line 92
Hortonworks distribution
  Oozie, configuring in 1-6
Hue
  configuring 19-23
  installing 19-23
  URL 20
Hue 3.9.0
  URL 38

I

input and output events, Dataset
  current(int n) 84, 85
  daysInMonth(int n) 85
  hoursInDay(int n) 85
  latest(int n) 85, 86
  parameters 84

J

job.properties file 112, 113
job property file
  defining 46-48

K

Kerberos principle
  URL 138

L

Lambda architecture
  URL 59

M

MapReduce jobs
  job.properties file 56
  running 56
  running, from Oozie 54

Thank you for buying
Apache Oozie Essentials

About Packt Publishing

Packt, pronounced 'packed', published its first book, *Mastering phpMyAdmin for Effective MySQL Management*, in April 2004, and subsequently continued to specialize in publishing highly focused books on specific technologies and solutions.

Our books and publications share the experiences of your fellow IT professionals in adapting and customizing today's systems, applications, and frameworks. Our solution-based books give you the knowledge and power to customize the software and technologies you're using to get the job done. Packt books are more specific and less general than the IT books you have seen in the past. Our unique business model allows us to bring you more focused information, giving you more of what you need to know, and less of what you don't.

Packt is a modern yet unique publishing company that focuses on producing quality, cutting-edge books for communities of developers, administrators, and newbies alike. For more information, please visit our website at www.packtpub.com.

About Packt Open Source

In 2010, Packt launched two new brands, Packt Open Source and Packt Enterprise, in order to continue its focus on specialization. This book is part of the Packt Open Source brand, home to books published on software built around open source licenses, and offering information to anybody from advanced developers to budding web designers. The Open Source brand also runs Packt's Open Source Royalty Scheme, by which Packt gives a royalty to each open source project about whose software a book is sold.

Writing for Packt

We welcome all inquiries from people who are interested in authoring. Book proposals should be sent to author@packtpub.com. If your book idea is still at an early stage and you would like to discuss it first before writing a formal book proposal, then please contact us; one of our commissioning editors will get in touch with you.

We're not just looking for published authors; if you have strong technical skills but no writing experience, our experienced editors can help you develop a writing career, or simply get some additional reward for your expertise.

Apache Kafka

ISBN: 978-1-78216-793-8 Paperback: 88 pages

Set up Apache Kafka clusters and develop custom message producers and consumers using practical, hands-on examples

1. Write custom producers and consumers with message partition techniques.

2. Integrate Kafka with Apache Hadoop and Storm for use cases such as processing streaming data.

3. Provide an overview of Kafka tools and other contributions that work with Kafka in areas such as logging, packaging, and so on.

Mastering Apache Spark

ISBN: 978-1-78398-714-6 Paperback: 318 pages

Gain expertise in processing and storing data by using advanced techniques with Apache Spark

1. Explore the integration of Apache Spark with third party applications such as H20, Databricks and Titan.

2. Evaluate how Cassandra and Hbase can be used for storage.

3. An advanced guide with a combination of instructions and practical examples to extend the most up-to date Spark functionalities.

Please check **www.PacktPub.com** for information on our titles

Apache Hive Essentials

ISBN: 978-1-78355-857-5   Paperback: 208 pages

Immerse yourself on a fantastic journey to discover the attributes of big data by using Hive

1. Discover how Hive can coexist and work with other tools in the Hadoop ecosystem to create big data solutions.

2. Grasp the skills needed, learn the best practices, and avoid the pitfalls in writing efficient Hive queries to analyze the big data.

3. Create an environment to analyze big data using practical, example-oriented scenarios.

Learning Apache Mahout Classification

ISBN: 978-1-78355-495-9   Paperback: 130 pages

Build and personalize your own classifiers using Apache Mahout

1. Explore the different types of classification algorithms available in Apache Mahout.

2. Create and evaluate your own ready-to-use classification models using real world datasets.

3. A practical guide to problems faced in classification with concepts explained in an easy-to-understand manner.

Please check **www.PacktPub.com** for information on our titles